YOUR
KITTEN
Choice and Care

Domestic Black

Balinese

YOUR
KITTEN
Choice and Care

Written by Paddy Cutts
Photographs by Animals Unlimited/Paddy Cutts

FOREWORD BY BRIAN DOYLE

H HOWELL
BOOK HOUSE
New York

© Copyright 1989 by Merehurst Limited

First American Edition, 1990

Howell Book House
Macmillan Publishing Company
866 Third Avenue, New York, NY 10022
Collier Macmillan Canada, Inc.

ISBN 0-87605-839-X

Library of Congress Cataloging-in-Publication Data

Cutts, Paddy,
    Your kitten: choice and care/written by Paddy Cutts;
photographs by Animals Unlimited/Paddy Cutts;
foreword by Brian Doyle — 1st American ed.
        p.   cm.
    ISBN 0-87605-839-X
    1. Kittens, I. Title
SF447.C88   1990
636.8'07—dc20   89-39576
                                                            CIP

Macmillan books are available at special discounts
for bulk purchases for sales promotions, premiums, fund-raising,
or educational use. For details contact:

Special Sales Director
Macmillan Publishing Company
866 Third Avenue
New York, N.Y. 10022

10 9 8 7 6 5 4 3 2 1

Printed in Portugal by Printer Portuguesa Industria LDA

CONTENTS

British Silver Tabby

ACKNOWLEDGEMENTS

There have been many kind people who have helped me to compile this book, and to whom due acknowledgement must be made.

Audrey Cutts, my Mum, what would I have done without the wonderful computer machine that you bought me as a Christmas present? Not forgetting Murray Thomas, without whose help I would never have fathomed out how to use it; Edward Young, FCIS, for his assistance in proofing the text, and ensuring that I made as few grammatical errors as possible; the late Peter Cronin, BVSc, MRCVS, who was my excellent veterinary surgeon, and who helped me to keep my cats fit and healthy, and who was kind enough to proof the 'Ailments and First Aid' chapter; Rosemary Alger, for her help with the general content of this book and her most expert advice on breeding and the rearing of kittens. She was, as usual, a tower of strength when I needed it the most! Barbara Harrington, Secretary of the GCCF Cat Welfare Liaison Committee, for her most helpful advice on many aspects, but particularly for imparting to me her knowledge of the Siamese breed; Sal Marsh, BA Hons, for bearing with me, and for all her help in making the picture selection. She knows my photo-library as well as I do, but a 'fresh eye' can make all the difference when choosing the best pictures; Brian Doyle, for his most flattering foreword!

FOREWORD

If you belong to the British cat fancy you will need no introduction to Paddy Cutts. If, on the other hand, you have bought this book as a newcomer to kitten or cat owning, perhaps I can make the introduction for you. Paddy Cutts is, first and foremost, an out-and-out ailurophile. She loves other animals, but cats are her real love. But, having said that, Paddy is not blinded by her feelings for these graceful creatures. She is deeply concerned for their welfare and frequent ill-treatment by mankind. Somehow, in between her busy life as a top animal photographer and writer, she manages to slot in time to help to rehome distressed cats, rescued cats, or any cat she hears of that is believed to be unhappy in its current environment. That is why you will find that her message in this book is a fervent plea that you do not buy a kitten unless you are fully aware of, and prepared to take on the responsibility of becoming an owner. Paddy's experience as a breeder and life-long cat owner have given her the necessary practical knowledge to be able to write this book. Her natural love and empathy for the cat give her the right to do so.

BRIAN DOYLE
Editor, *Cats* magazine (UK)

Domestic Tabby-and-white

A NEW KITTEN

Kittens, probably more than any other domestic pet, are so attractive and appealing to humans that it is all too easy to give one a home without thinking of the consequences. Children, particularly at Christmas or birthday times, can be very persuasive and their parents may all too readily give in to their constant pleas for a pet kitten, without realising just what they are letting themselves and their families in for!

A popular misconception is that cats are totally independent: that they do not need to be taken for walks like dogs; nor do they need the special cages or containers necessary for smaller pets, such as mice, hamsters or gerbils; that they are clean little animals, and use the garden for their toilet, so all one has to do is open a tin of cat food and they will be happy with the minimum of attention. If this is your idea of a pet kitten, then read no further, as no self-respecting feline would wish to take up residence in your home, and if circumstances caused it to do so, would probably not stay there very long!

Cats do not vary in size to anything like the same extent as dogs do, but the type or breed of kitten that you finally choose should be the result of serious research and contemplation. Well cared for, and barring accidents, your kitten will mature into a fully grown cat and could live for sixteen years or more. If it is to grow into a happy, well-adjusted and sociable family pet, you will have to think about doing more than just using a can opener once a day. However, your efforts will be well rewarded, so if the acquisition of a kitten is your ideal, please read on, as this book is aimed at helping you select the right feline for your home and family.

Pedigree or Non-pedigree?

There are various reasons for wanting a kitten. You may want only a companionable pet, or have the higher aspirations of owning, or indeed breeding for yourself, a top show-winning pedigree cat. So what is the difference?

A pedigree cat, by definition, may only be described by this term if its parents were registered with one of the many governing organisations that have been set up in various countries to authenticate feline parentage, normally for four generations. With the help of modern-day computerised records, it is now very simple to trace a pedigree kitten's ancestors back many, many generations and it is not unusual to find that you know more about your kitten's history than your own!

But what is to be gained by this knowledge?

These pedigree cats show how the breeds vary in size:
(left) Korat; (right) British Red Spotted Tabby

Longhairs need patient grooming

Firstly, in most cases temperament is genetically inherited. By both seeing and knowing the parentage of your kitten, you will have a very good idea of the sort of cat it will become. Equally, size, colour and personality can all be gleaned from seeing the parents. The pedigree papers will often show champions and grand champions in its details, but impressive as they may seem, these facts alone will not always help you to select the best pet for your household.

Selecting the Right Pedigree Breed for You

Although cats may have the reputation of being independent, they are really quite demanding and the various breeds have their own needs. They all have good points, and a few bad ones too, so you must think seriously about what you are looking for in your pet, the time you will be able to make available to it, and your own lifestyle.

Pedigree cats are generally recognised as belonging to five different groupings. Each breed, and, in some cases, even colour variations, can produce quite different temperaments and characters. Later in this book a detailed description of each breed is given, and this should be read thoroughly before you decide on the breed most suitable for you. It is of equal importance to consider personality as well as the physical attributes of any breed, as some can tend to be more demanding than others!

Generally, the groups can be summarised as follows:

Longhairs
These are usually quiet in voice and gentle in temperament, but will require regular, and often daily, grooming. They do not shed fur any more than other varieties but, due to its length, any loose hair on the carpet tends to be more obvious! They are not usually as adventurous, or demanding, as their 'foreign' relatives and will not object if they have to be left alone while you go to work.

British Shorthairs
Temperamentally, this group is similar to their Longhaired relatives, but they do have a tendency to become *very* large! Their coats, although short, are very dense and plushy, and so will also require regular grooming.

Foreign Shorthairs
These are quite a mixed bunch, few of which have the same characteristics. They are generally lively and intelligent cats that do not like to be left on their own. They include such breeds as the Abyssinian, the Korat and the Foreign Black. Most, except for the rex varieties, have sleek, close-lying, short coats that do not require excessive grooming.

*A litter of eight-week-old Longhair kittens: even at this
age their coats will need careful grooming*

The Chinchilla is a magical-looking Longhair

Burmese

These can be summed up quite easily – lovable hooligans that are not for the faint-hearted! They are an intelligent breed, and will try to get into everything and anything, often to their detriment. It is inadvisable to have only one Burmese if you are out at work, as they dislike being left on their own and can tend to be destructive if they become bored. They are very loving, almost to the point of smothering you, and will demand constant attention while you are at home.

Siamese

These are probably the most instantly recognisable pedigree breed, with long elegant bodies and distinctive markings. Like the Burmese, their main drawbacks are their inquisitive intelligence coupled with their dislike of being left alone for any great length of time – and Siamese also have much the loudest voices of any known feline breed! However, they respond well to discipline, and most will take readily to the idea of a collar and lead if you wish to take them for a walk!

Giving a Home to a Non-pedigree Kitten

Do not lightly dismiss the idea of taking in a kitten of uncertain parentage; such kittens will become just as delightful and friendly pets as the more costly pedigree models and, in many instances, will look just as glamorous!

'Moggy' cats come in a multitude of colours and with different lengths of fur: sleek black cats, fluffy tortoiseshells, classic tabbies, marmalades and gingers, tortoiseshell-tabbies . . . the possibilities are endless, and each will have its own special attraction for the right owner.

The drawbacks are that you will not know much about the cat's inherited temperament, but if you take a kitten at about six to eight weeks old, you should find that it will settle in very quickly. Do, however, make sure that the kitten is quite healthy and is not going to involve you in expensive veterinary treatment. If you are unsure, get a vet to give your prospective kitten the 'once over', to put your mind at rest.

Taking in an Older Cat

There are many unwanted adult cats that need good homes, and you may find the idea of taking in such a cat attractive. The advantages to this are that the cat will most likely already have been neutered and inoculated, and you will also be able to see its character and temperament. It is not just moggies that need to be rehomed, so if you find the cost of a pedigree kitten above your means, do think about taking in an adult cat of your chosen variety.

Burmese – lovable hooligans

Non-pedigree kitten

Male or Female?

Unless it is your intention to breed from your kitten, there is very little difference between the sexes once they have been neutered. A male kitten will usually grow into a larger adult cat, so this fact may sway your decision; some people prefer a little lady cat, whilst others prefer to own a more 'macho'-looking neutered male. The choice is really one of personal preference, but there are a few points that should be considered:

1 With either sex, the kitten will have to be neutered at about six months old and this operation is cheaper for a male than a female. It is also possible that you will have to take your female back to the vet about a fortnight after the operation to have stitches removed, unless dissolving stitches have been used.
2 If you do not have your female neutered, you will have a feline population explosion on your hands within a short space of time! You will be unlikely to find good homes for all the kittens.
3 Even when neutered, a male cat may be more likely to spray than a female. Some breeds are more prone to this territorial behaviour than others.

One Kitten or Two?

Unless you already own a cat, it is sensible to acquire two kittens at the same time and for very good reasons!

1 They will be company for each other and this will ease the settling-in period when they first come to their new home. One kitten could be frightened on its own.
2 In your absence from home, they will each have a 'little friend' to play with. This could have a beneficial effect on your carpets and furnishings as the kittens are unlikely to become bored with each other's company and so will not feel the need to destroy your home while you are out!
3 When you go away on holiday, you will most likely put your cat into a cattery. This can be a lonely time for a feline, but a known companion will make the experience much more pleasant.
4 You may not always feel in the mood to play with your cat; two together will help to solve this problem!
5 Two cats can be double the pleasure to own; the games they will play, and the antics they can get up to, are quite likely to make you consider getting rid of the television set.

Two kittens can be better than one

Females are often more slender than the males

A bulky male of the same breed (Blue Burmese)

In Conclusion

There is a popular bumper sticker that reads 'A puppy is for life, not just for Christmas', and the purchase or acquisition of a kitten should be considered in the same light. Please do take the time and effort to think carefully before you give a kitten or cat a place in your home. It will be with you for a long, long time. Some of the points raised in this book are actually designed to put you off certain breeds which may not be suitable for your household – surely it is better to be warned off by certain traits and characteristics, rather than end up sending a kitten back to its breeder, or to a 'pound', just because you did not realise the demands that it could put upon you?

WHERE TO FIND YOUR KITTEN

There are various ways of acquiring a kitten, and these are largely dictated by your choice of a recognised, pedigree breed, a kitten of unknown parentage, or giving a home to a grown cat. Whatever your decision, a pet shop is *not* the place to go. Fortunately, few reputable pet shops actually stock kittens and puppies, as they realise that a shop is not a suitable environment for such young, vulnerable and intelligent animals.

The few shops that do sell livestock of this kind rarely know much about them. Most have probably bought their animals from a dubious source and will charge a highly inflated price, often for an uninoculated kitten that has been taken from its mother at far too young an age and, if a pedigree breed, does not have authenticated papers! So where should you look to find your kitten?

Buying a Pedigree Kitten

Once you have decided which breed and colour of kitten you would like, the first step is to contact a reputable breeder. You may perhaps know a friend who has a cat of the breed you are looking for and who would be able to recommend that cat's breeder as a reliable source of happy, healthy kittens. Personal recommendation is one of the best ways to track down any service or commodity, but if this is not possible, there are various ways to find a suitable breeder.

First, try asking the local veterinary surgeries, as any good cat breeder will need to use the services of a vet, if only to have kittens inoculated.

Various weekly and monthly cat magazines are available, and most publish a breeder's directory as well as advertisements of kittens for sale. These magazines also list any forthcoming cat shows and a visit to one of these will enable you to meet the breeders and see some of their cats. Remember that cat shows are really only a shop window for breeders to exhibit their stock, and few shows will allow the sale of kittens direct to the public.

Most breeds of cat will have their own, specialist breed club, the majority of which run a kitten list. A telephone call to the club secretary, or local regional representative, should leave you with a list of people to contact, who have kittens for sale.

It is quite likely that you may have to travel some distance to look at the kittens. If you have decided on one of the more popular breeds, such as Siamese, you may find that there are several breeders in your locality, but if your preference is for one of the rarer varieties, you must not expect to find a breeder on your doorstep. The kitten you choose is going to be part of your family for a good many years, so do spend some time and effort in visiting various breeders before you make your ultimate decision.

Do, by all means, go and visit several litters of kittens, although it is inadvisable to see more than one litter on the same day; you could, albeit inadvertently, carry a virus from one household to another. Remember, young kittens are most vulnerable to infection.

You will most likely be invited to view a litter of kittens when they are about six to eight weeks old, and prior to the visit the breeder will probably want to question you thoroughly. This is to make sure that, for both your benefits, there is a suitable kitten available and that you can offer it the right sort of home. So you should be prepared to answer the following types of questions:

1 What are your domestic arrangements, size of home and number of children?
2 Do you go out to work and, if so, will there be somebody at home during the daytime?
3 Will the kitten have access to a garden, or will it be confined to an indoor area?
4 Do you have any other animals?
5 How did you hear of the breeder?
6 The reason for wanting a kitten. Is it your intention to breed from it or show it?
7 Is the kitten for yourself, or are you buying it as a present for somebody else?
8 Do you know anything about the particular breed, such as habits and temperament?
9 Are you aware of the price of a pedigree kitten?

Contacting the Breeder

For the vast majority of breeders, their cats are a hobby, with kittens being an added bonus. Many will also have full or part-time jobs and perhaps a family to bring up (apart from their feline one!). Unlike dog breeding, which is often a more commercial and profitable concern, cat breeders are most

Unlike the typical dog breeder with kennels in an
outbuilding, cat breeders usually share their homes with
their cats and kittens

likely to keep their kittens in their homes, as opposed to in a specially built cattery.

There are also some breeders who may keep several cats for breeding and so, most sensibly, will not find it practical to keep them all indoors, and may have some housed in cat houses and runs outside.

Whichever of the two situations you find, remember that cat breeders are very busy people, so always telephone first to make an appointment to visit – you would not appreciate complete strangers turning up at your home unannounced, so afford the same respect to the poor cat breeder!

Once you have made an appointment, do keep to the agreed date and time: few things are more infuriating than to agree a fixed appointment and then find that the viewer fails to turn up. If you are delayed for any reason, telephone and let the breeder know – this is only a common courtesy, after all.

Visiting the Breeder

In case you have not been forewarned, do not wear your best clothes when visiting the kittens; silk stockings and designer clothes will not impress either the breeder or the kittens and the latters' sharp claws could result in you being somewhat out of pocket as well! Wear sensible clothing, and preferably long trousers, as kittens have the unfortunate habit of trying to climb up human legs. Trousers will save you from being scratched!

If your choice of kitten is to be a family affair, do let the breeder know how many of you are likely to arrive: most breeders will want to meet the whole family and it is nice to know in advance the number of cups of coffee that may be required!

Especially if you have children, do not treat the visit to the breeder as you would a day out at the zoo. It's nice to meet the cats, and see the kittens, but try not to overstay your welcome and do not take all the neighbourhood children along for a treat. It is equally important to tell any children that they must be on their best behaviour and should not run around. Not all breeders have children of their own, and a loud or clumsy child could easily upset the kittens, not to mention your chances of being considered as a suitable owner!

Do not be offended if you are not actually allowed to touch the kittens or, if you are, that you are first asked to wash your hands with diluted disinfectant. This is no slur on your personal hygiene. An uninoculated kitten can contract an infection very easily, so it is only a sensible precaution.

During your initial visit, you will be asked even more questions and, again, these are just to ensure that the kitten will be going to the right sort of home and environment. Do not expect to take your kitten home that day. You will most likely be asked to go home and consider this important step before you make your final decision. Be wary of any breeder who is prepared to sell you a kitten immediately, as there is most likely a good, and not pleasant, reason for selling in this way.

If you decide to reserve a kitten, you might be asked for a deposit. This will leave you in the knowledge that your chosen kitten will be kept for you, while the breeder has a token amount of money that, in the event that you change your mind, will pay the cost of re-advertising the kitten.

Animal Sanctuaries and Rescue Centres

Taking in a kitten or cat from a sanctuary or rescue centre will still involve you in all the above questioning. These places are dealing, every day, with unwanted cats and kittens, and will want to be just as sure as any breeder would that this time the cat is going to a good, suitable and stable home. Do not be surprised if such organisations also insist on a visit to your home before letting any animal into your possession. Most well-regarded charities insist on such a visit, so do not be offended!

Your local 'phone directory will list the various rescue centres in your area, and a visit to one of these will reveal some most pathetic animals. Do not be put off, as most will grow into quite beautiful cats with a little love and attention. This is one situation where it is probably better not to take young, cat-loving children with you. They could easily be quite upset at the sight of so many unwanted moggies, and are quite likely to encourage you to make a snap decision, or, even worse, to take in several cats!

As with a pedigree cat, think about the responsibilities of sensible cat ownerhsip, and do not make a decision until the whole family is in agreement. Depending on the time of year, these centres will quite likely have young kittens in need of new homes, so they can be a most useful way of finding a nice, healthy, little kitten. Few centres will allow a kitten to leave their premises uninoculated and so you can rest assured that the kitten is healthy.

You will not often be asked actually to pay for a kitten from a rescue centre (apart, possibly, from the cost of inoculations), but it is a common gesture to make a contribution to the charity involved – this will help them to keep up their good work!

During the spring and summer months, your local paper will most likely carry advertisements such as 'kittens: free to good homes'. When visiting any of these litters, take the same point of view that you would with a litter of pedigree cats. Short of a stud fee, these kittens have cost just as much to raise and feed as pedigree cats, but the owner is unlikely to charge a price for the kittens.

An adult cat may be worth considering

Adopting an Older Cat

There are many reasons for taking in a more adult cat which can still make a wonderful feline companion. Some people think, quite correctly, that as there is a huge population of unwanted cats around, one of these should be offered a permanent home. Equally, more elderly folk could find that although they long for a feline friend, a kitten would prove too much to handle and so they would prefer a cat at a more stately age! Whatever your reason for wanting one, a rescued adult can prove a delightful choice.

Both cat clubs and rescue centres can help you in your quest. Most clubs have a rehoming list, as well as one of kittens for sale. They are thus likely to be able to put you in touch with somebody who has available the pedigree breed of your choice.

The main difference in acquiring a rehomer is that there is less chance of knowing the parentage and the temperament that has been inherited. Think carefully, and take a good look at the cat before accepting such a responsibility.

WHAT TO LOOK FOR

It is best, wherever possible, to buy your kitten direct from a reputable breeder, who will be unlikely to sell you anything other than a happy, healthy kitten. News travels fast in the cat fancy, and no good breeder would wish to risk his or her reputation by selling a kitten that was not 100 per cent healthy, inoculated and ready to go to its new home.

You should be allowed to see all the kittens in the litter, as well as the mother cat and any other cats in the household. This should give you an indication of the size, type and temperament that your kitten will develop in maturity. Not all cat breeders have their own stud cat, so you may not be able to see the father. However, you will be able to tell a lot about the kitten by watching its behaviour towards its mother and siblings.

General Points to Look For

1 All the kittens should be friendly and extrovert, and seem pleased to receive their visitors. Some kittens will have stronger personalities than others, and a little shyness at this age is unlikely to last for very long. However, any kitten that cowers away from humans, or runs away and hides, may develop personality problems as it grows older.

It is important for kittens to be handled by their breeder from birth onwards and any kittens that are frightened of people at six weeks old, have probably not had enough early handling and attention from the breeder. Do not buy a kitten like

Healthy kittens have bright eyes and a clean, glossy coat

this, as it is unlikely to develop into a sociable family pet.

2 The eyes should be bright and clear, with no sign of the haws up (see the Glossary). There should be no discharge or sign of weepiness. The standard for some breeds requires very short noses, as in most longhaired varieties, but this should never be so extreme as to cause continually weeping eyes.

3 The nose should be clean and wet, but without snuffles, sneezes or any discharge.

4 The ears should be clean. Dark brown waxy secretions, accompanied by persistent scratching or shaking of the head, could be symptomatic of ear-mite infestation.

5 The coat should be clean and bright. If the kitten is seen to be scratching a lot, it may have fleas or some other type of external parasite.

6 All the kittens should have a clean and pleasant smell about them and the litter tray should not be seen to contain any sign of diarrhoea or loose motions. Check the tray frequently to be sure.

Specialist Points to Check on

If you are buying a pedigree kitten with a view either to showing or breeding, it is important to make sure that you select one that conforms to the standard of points as closely as possible. Make it quite clear to the breeder, at the first meeting, that you are looking for a show or breeding quality kitten. Each breed has its own standards, and you should familiarise yourself with these (see the List of Breeds), but general faults can be of any of the following:

1 **Tail faults** The required length and shape of the tail vary from breed to breed, but a tail fault should never be present, either visible or otherwise. The tail is quite a fragile part of a kitten's anatomy and should not be roughly handled. However, it is a good idea to make a final check by gently running your thumb and forefinger along the length of the tail, from the base of the spine to the tail tip. If there is any knob or bump at any point, or the continuation from the spine is

Pedigree kittens conforming to standard

not straight, this kitten is not suitable for either breeding or the show bench.

2 **Eye colour** All kittens are born with blue eyes, so do not be upset if, at six weeks old, the kittens do not have the correct eye colour for their breed! At about eight weeks the eye colour will start to change, and by twelve weeks, in most breeds, it should give a good indication of what the adult hue will be.

3 **Coat colour, length and patterning** Firstly, do remember that the coat colour in most breeds will look quite different in a kitten than in an adult cat. Longhaired kittens do not have a full coat until they are several months old and so you will have to trust your breeder's choice of the kitten with the best coat. The main faults to look for are any patches of white in the solid, self or tortie breeds (this can be difficult in some colours, so try comparing any suspect patches with a piece of clean, white cotton wool). With those breeds, such as Siamese, Colourpoints and Birmans, that have very specific standards for the coat pattern, the markings must not be mismatched or uneven, and should be restricted to the head, paws and tail only.

4 **Jaw alignment** It is considered a severe fault for a kitten to be either overshot or undershot (see the Glossary), and the alignment of the upper and lower jaws should be perfectly straight and even.

Let us hope you will now feel content that the kittens are healthy and suitable for your requirements, and also that the breeder is honest and has a genuine concern that the kittens are sold only to good homes. At this point, price will be discussed, if it has not been mentioned before. Many people do not have the vaguest idea how much a pedigree animal costs, and it can come as a bit of a shock!

Most breeders will suggest that you 'sleep on it' for twenty-four hours before making your final decision to buy. This affords both of you a 'cooling off' period and if, for whatever reason, one or other of you decides that the sale should not go through, it is so much easier to say so over the telephone than face to face!

If either of you has any qualms whatsoever, the sale should not proceed. Be honest with each other and discuss any problems or worries openly.

If you decide to go ahead with the purchase, you will be seeing quite a lot of both the breeder and your chosen kitten over the next few weeks! On the first visit, you will most likely have forgotten to ask some questions, but these can be dealt with before your kitten is ready to leave its mother at twelve weeks old.

You may be asked to leave a deposit confirming that the kitten is reserved for you. This is not at all unreasonable.

Many breeders feel that any prospective owners should get to know their kitten well, and are quite likely to suggest that you make a regular weekly visit. This will help you and your kitten to get to know each other, and will make the transition to its new home that much easier, as the kitten will already know and trust you and your family.

Over these weeks, you should make sure of the following points:

1 That the kitten will be fully inoculated at least three or four days before you take it to its new home. If you visit the kitten after the inoculation has been administered, do not worry if it seems a little snuffly, or sneezes. This is a quite normal reaction to the vaccine, although not all kittens will be affected.

2 That the papers (see the Glossary) are all in order, and that you have a signed pedigree certifying the parentage. If you have bought a kitten for show or breeding purposes, you should also be given a transfer form, signed by the breeder, with a space for your own signature. This will enable you officially to transfer the ownership of the kitten. Do make sure that this is sent off to the relevant cat council without delay. Some breeders may also give you the registration document, but most prefer to keep this on file for their own reference.

If you are buying a 'pet-quality' kitten, you should also receive the pedigree, transfer form and inoculation certificate, and this is for a good reason. If the breeder does not consider that the kitten should be bred from, or indeed shown, and these points have been accepted by both parties when the sale is agreed, the kitten will most likely have been registered on the 'non-active' register. This means that it cannot be bred from without the breeder's authorisation and the payment of an additional fee to the governing council. This is sensible, as no well-respected breeder wants to perpetuate unwanted faults in the line of breeding, although these kittens may be shown.

Some pet-quality kittens may be registered under the 'declared only' category, and these may not be shown or bred from without the breeder's permission for the alteration of status.

3 That the kitten has received a course of worming tablets.

Lastly . . .

Do keep in contact with the breeder, who will have spent a good deal of time and effort (not to mention money) in raising the kittens, to ensure that they have had the best possible start in life. It is now your responsibility to continue with this good work, so that your kitten develops into a happy and healthy adult cat. If you have any worries, problems or queries, do contact the breeder first, who will most likely be able to put your mind at rest – but do not make this a daily routine! With the best will in the world, patience will wear thin if you telephone too often. However, for the first few days at least, questions will probably arise and most breeders do not consider that their responsibility towards their kittens ends as soon as you walk out of the door with it.

If, for any reason, your circumstances change, and you are no longer able to keep the kitten, let the breeder know. Many breeders will offer to take the kitten (or cat) back, but if this is not possible, most will probably know of a suitable new home.

Equally important, do advise the breeder if you move house, and send a change of address card. It is difficult to keep records up to date if you do not know that an owner has moved home!

BRINGING YOUR KITTEN HOME

A new kitten arriving in your home can be likened to a new baby being brought home for the first time. There is much preparation to be done and, to a certain extent, your usual household routines will have to be altered to accommodate the new arrival. It is a traumatic experience for any small creature to be taken away from its mother and brought into a new environment, but with a little preparation and foresight, this transition can easily be made as pleasant as possible.

Preparing for the New Arrival
There are certain items of equipment that you will need, and these should be bought in advance. These are a litter tray and litter, food and water bowls, a cosy bed and bedding and some toys to keep the new kitten amused.

Kitten on a litter tray

Enclosed litter tray

Selection of food and water bowls

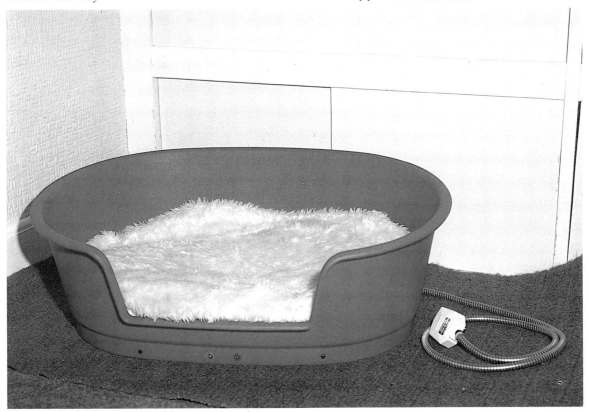

Heated bed: the flex is protected by a metal conduit

If you have bought a pedigree kitten from a breeder, a diet sheet should have been provided so that you can purchase, in advance, the type of food that the kitten is used to. If this is not the case, it is best to start the kitten on one of the proprietary brands of kitten food, as these have been designed to give a young cat the best nourishment during its development (see Feeding your Kitten).

Most specially bred and pedigree kittens have been reared in a warm environment, so if you acquire your kitten in winter, and do not have good heating, think about buying a heated bed or pad to keep your kitten warm.

At this stage it is also a good idea to register with a local vet, if you do not already have one, explaining to him or her the age and breed of the kitten that you are to bring home. If you live in a city, you will find that most veterinary practices are used to small animals, but in country areas where there are large farming communities, it is well worth shopping around to find a veterinarian who is a 'cat man or woman'.

Your kitten should have been inoculated against FIE (feline infectious enteritis) and cat 'flu before you bring it home, but in the event that it has not received these important inoculations, arrange with the vet to have them administered very soon.

It is also a good idea to ask for the kitten to have a thorough check-up, to make sure that it is in the peak of health before you bring it home: this is especially important if you have another cat or other animals, as infections can spread very quickly and treatment is often costly.

Of equal importance is to ensure that any other cats resident in your household have also been inoculated at least two weeks before you bring your new kitten home.

Transporting Your Kitten
The chances are that having collected your new kitten, you may have to travel some distance to reach home. This may mean using rail, road, or even air transportation and for a small animal this can be a frightening experience the first time.

Cardboard boxes are all well and good for a short distance, but are really not strong enough to contain an inquisitive and nervous kitten for very long. During the course of your kitten's life, you will have to transport it for many reasons. There will be the annual trip to the vet, for inoculations; perhaps to the boarding cattery when you go on holiday; you might even wish to show the kitten and a good-quality carrying basket will prove a sound investment.

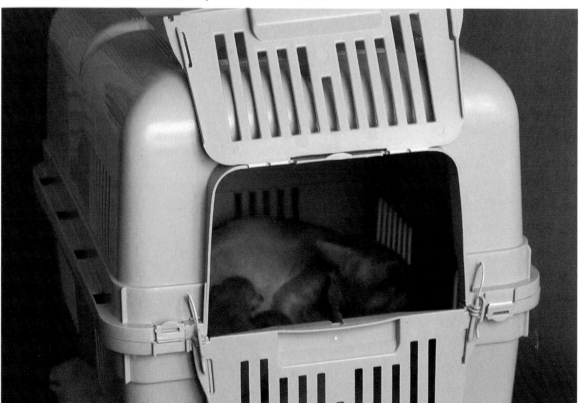

A good quality carrying basket

Try to buy one that will make the kitten feel secure and happy. There are many different models on the market, but depending on your need and the amount of usage, it is not necessary to buy the most expensive one! Cat-carrying baskets come in all shapes and sizes, from a simple wicker picnic hamper type, to the most sophisticated models that meet with airline regulations for air transportation.

Somewhere between the two extremes you are sure to find the right one to suit your requirements. The most important features to look for are good, secure and sturdy door fastenings; adequate ventilation; a window, or similar space, so that the kitten can look out; and a good, strong carrying handle.

If you are thinking of travelling with your kitten frequently, then do get it used to its carrying basket as soon as possible, so that it will not be nervous on any future journeys.

There are some excellent baskets that literally come apart at the seams so that they can be converted into two sleeping beds in just a few seconds. Look round your local pet store or the trade stands at a cat show. You will be surprised at just how many ways there are to transport your kitten in both style and comfort! But do remember to buy a carrier big enough to carry a full size cat – your kitten will grow!

Just one word of warning. Do not borrow your neighbour's cat basket unless you are sure that it has been thoroughly disinfected. It is so easy to pass on an infection and most pet owners only ever use their basket to take a sick cat to the vet.

Settling Your Kitten into its New Home
Most kittens settle quite readily into a new home and will be fascinated by all the new areas to explore. Take one step at a time, and confine the kitten to the main area that it will be using within your home, which is most likely to be the living room. A small kitten can be quite intimidated by large areas, so a little at a time is the best way for it to find its way around a strange house.

Although it is tempting to buy a kitten at Christmas time, or as a birthday present, this should be avoided. Parties and celebrations are all very well for the usual occupants of the household, but to a little kitten such festivities could be quite frightening, particularly if it is the centre of attention.

The kindest way to settle a new kitten into your home is when you have ample time to spend with it. If you are at work during the week, then try to make this time at a weekend, perhaps even taking a day off on either side, in order to make sure your new arrival feels secure and contented. For a larger family with young children, try to make this introduction when there is a quiet time in the home,

such as when the children are away at school and there will be the least amount of noise and activity.

Bearing all this in mind, and assuming you have now brought your new kitten home, try to observe the following procedure. First, show the kitten where it can find its food and water bowls and, most important, its litter tray. (It is a good idea to put your new kitten on its litter tray as soon as you arrive home, as it may well need to use it immediately!) Try to put these in a place that is convenient for both you and the kitten, and always place the kitten on its litter tray immediately after feeding.

If the kitten has an 'accident', do not scold it, as it will not understand, but simply put it back on its tray, so that it knows the correct procedure.

Cats are creatures of habit and do not like unnecessary domestic upheaval, so make sure that your kitten can find these items in the same place each day! Initially, try to use the brand or type of cat litter that the kitten is used to. Many varieties are available, some of which are quite powdery, and these can cause irritation if the kitten is not used to the product. It is not unknown for a new owner to complain to the kitten's breeder that it is showing all the signs of cat 'flu, when it is really only displaying the effects of a dusty irritant that causes sneezing and weeping eyes – central heating, coal dust and gas or oil fumes can also cause the same reaction in some cats!

Gradually, over a period of days, introduce your kitten to those rooms that you are happy for it to enter. There may be some areas, for one reason or another, that you wish to put out of bounds. Start as you mean to go on, making this quite clear at the outset to the kitten, and keep the doors to these rooms firmly closed. Once a kitten has discovered a new room, it will be forever miaowing until it is allowed back in.

Kittens are very inquisitive little creatures and this can sometimes lead to tragedy. There are so many interesting items of domestic equipment to be found in any home, that they find it difficult to resist the temptation of making a thorough investigation. If you think of your new kitten as a mischievous human toddler, you will begin to realise what you are going to have to cope with, at least for the first few months.

The kitchen is an area where, for a kitten, the most dangerous appliances are to be found. Cookers, hob units, food processors, and such like, should never be left unattended when in use if the kitten has access to the kitchen. The warmth of an oven, the smell of a meal cooking, or the steam rising from a boiling pan can all prove an irresistible temptation and could lead to tragic consequences.

Washing machines and tumble driers are even

more dangerous and should be operated with the greatest care. The best way to prevent an accident with these machines is to make a head count of any animals in the home before switching such appliances on, making sure that this becomes a house rule that your entire family is aware of.

Electrical and telephone wires are easily chewed through, so it is a good idea to keep an eye on these if your kitten proves to be a 'phantom chewer'. Not all cats are attracted to cables, but to the owners of those that are, it can become embarrassing to have to call out a telephone engineer yet again because the 'phone is out-of-order!

Equally, it can somewhat disrupt the festive celebrations if your kitten chooses to chew through the wires of the Christmas tree lights just as you are about to carve the turkey. This has been known to happen and trying to find a duty vet, whilst administering mouth-to-mouth resuscitation to your kitten, can dampen the Christmas spirit considerably. The best idea, if you find that your kitten is a chewer, is to invest in some flexible conduit that it cannot manage to chew through – prevention is always better than cure!

This is all probably enough to scare you stiff, but look at it again: almost everything is advice you yourself would accept when looking after a toddler, and there is a bonus, in that kittens need no nappies!

Introducing Your Kitten to the Outside World

Depending on your acommodation and lifestyle, you may or may not be able to allow your kitten its freedom. City flat dwellers, without a garden, are unlikely to be able to afford their kitten a free-range life, but despite popular misconception, this is not at all cruel as long as the cat or kitten has known no other environment. However, if your cat is to have access to the outside world, there are several points to consider.

No kitten should be allowed to go outside, or encounter other outside cats, until it has been fully inoculated for at least a fortnight. It should also be given a few weeks to settle into its new home before being allowed to explore the big, wide world that lurks outside the back door. At first, let the kitten out only when you are there to supervise what it is up to. Cats are extremely territorial and if you do not already own a cat which has exerted its own rights to your garden, then the chances are that some local cat has laid claim to this territory, and will seriously resent the invasion of its patch by an 'intruder'.

The kitchen can be a perilous place

*Young kittens should not be allowed to climb trees
unsupervised*

No kitten should be allowed outside at all until inoculated

Entire toms (male cats) can be quite aggressive, even to a small kitten, so until your kitten has established its own ranking in the local feline community, it is sensible to watch all outdoor activities closely just in case it is attacked. As the kitten matures towards adulthood, you should find that it has been accepted as a permanent resident by the local cats and that your garden is now known to be off-limits, as it now has a full-time occupant to keep guard!

Even when such territorial rights have been ex-erted by your cat, it is still foolhardy to let it out at night. Most domestic cats, as opposed to feral ones, would much prefer to be tucked up in bed where it is safe and warm, than to be out having a night on the tiles. It is no less than pathetic, when taking an early morning stroll, to find some poor little feline piteously miaowing to be let back into its home.

The dark hours are also the time when your kitten is most likely to meet with a road accident and this, probably more than any other situation, is the one most likely to shorten a cat's life. There are ways to make your kitten realise that cars can be nasty creatures, and one of the best does sound somewhat unpleasant. Cruel to be kind is a good adage, and often a true one, so try putting your kitten in a small basket or container and place this underneath the engine of your car. With the handbrake on, and staying in neutral gear, start the engine and rev it up hard for a few seconds only. Naturally, this should not be tried until your kitten is well established at home and used to playing in the garden. The kitten will be very frightened but, in most cases, will have learned the hard way, and will be unlikely to want to encounter such a dreadful mechanical beast again.

It is rare for a cat that has been hit by a car, and survived, ever to want to venture near a road again, so this ploy can provide a very good lesson for a young cat.

Educate your kitten to be wary of the many dangers in life, and you are well on the way to becoming a sensible and responsible cat owner, enjoying all the benefits that can be gained from sharing your home with a feline companion.

If your kitten is to have free access to the garden, once it is safe for it to do so, you may find it convenient to install a cat flap, which will allow the kitten to come and go as it pleases and save you having to keep on opening and closing doors.

There are two basic types of flap, the simplest one having a two-way door that the kitten pushes against to open. The drawback to this is that if your kitten can get in and out, then so can all the other neighbourhood felines! A more sophisticated model incorporates a magnetic device that is attached to the cat's collar, which will only allow the flap to open for the authorised cat.

As your kitten gets older, you may not wish it to continue using an indoor litter tray. If the kitten has only ever used cat litter, it may be a little confused when you try to teach it to use the soil in the garden. Try putting some of its soiled litter on a patch of the garden that you would like it to use as a toilet, and place the kitten on this area each time it has been fed. It will soon realise what you want it to do, and within a few days you should be able to dispense with a daytime litter tray.

The cat flap should be locked at night, to keep the kitten safely indoors, so the litter tray should still be brought out in the evening and put in its usual place so that the kitten knows where to find it.

Last, and most important, if your kitten is to go outside at all, make sure that it is wearing a collar with an identity tag giving your name, address and telephone number. Never fit a dog collar on a cat, as there is no 'give' in them. Special collars are available that have been designed for cats, and these incorporate a small area of elastic. If the cat were

As a young tom kitten grows to maturity he is likely to have to face territorial battles

to get such a collar caught in a tree, the elastic would stretch and the cat would be able to escape safely from the situation. Do not put the cat's name on the identity tag, or a thief may more easily entice it away.

Introducing Your Kitten to Other Animals in the Home

Although it is tempting to spoil your new kitten when you first bring it home, this will make any existing pets jealous, so the golden rule is to make sure that you give to all of them the same amount of love and attention.

If you already own another cat, introduce the kitten to it gradually. Most adult cats will take to a small kitten quite readily, and will want to 'mother' the new addition to the family. If there is any problem and the resident cat hisses or spits at the kitten, try feeding them in the same room with their bowls close together: the sight and smell of food will usually make them forget about each other! Cats always wash after a meal and you will probably find that in no time at all they will be washing each other.

Collar and tag

Chinchilla kitten with an Irish Wolfhound

30

Another trick is to make both cat and kitten smell the same. Cats react strongly to scent, and your resident cat may find that the kitten smells unfamiliar and treat it as an intruder. If this seems to be the case, rub a little talcum powder, perfume, cologne, or whatever *you* normally smell of, into both their coats. You are not a threat to them, and if both cats smell of you, they will soon be acting like long lost friends. When you sit down in the evening, make sure that both cat and kitten are equally petted and stroked by both you and any members of the family. Never have the kitten on your lap if the resident cat does not also have a lap to sit on!

Introducing a kitten to a dog is somewhat different. If the kitten has been brought up with dogs, it will not be afraid and should take to your dog immediately. If your dog has never seen a kitten before, then watch its reaction carefully. Some breeds of dog are instinctively 'ratters', and may think that a small kitten is quarry to be pounced on or attacked. Until you are completely sure of your dog's behaviour towards the kitten, never leave the two of them together unless you, or a member of your family, are there to keep an eye on the proceedings.

The converse of this is more usually seen! Dogs do tend to be rather soppy creatures, and are more than likely to come off the worse from their first encounter with a kitten! Trusting animals that canines are, they will usually view the new kitten, have a good sniff and, just as they walk away –wallop – the kitten strikes out at the strange large beast, and you end up with a dog with a well-scratched nose! Kittens have a born instinct for survival and most definitely put 'number one' first!

Lastly, do not forget any smaller pets, be they feathered, furry, cold blooded or aquatic! Budgerigars, mice, rats, gerbils, hamsters and such like are natural prey to the feline species: either keep them in a 'no-go area', or keep the room that they live in well locked. Fish tanks should receive the same consideration: put a lid or wire cage over the aquarium, or you may well find that your new kitten is having a little snack when you are not looking –food caught fresh always tastes better!

Do not leave a cat alone in a room with a loose bird, and make sure the cat or kitten cannot get

Teach children to handle kittens gently

Sharing a bed

Kittens in their own bed

close enough to the bird's cage to terrorise it. Small birds have been known to die of fright in this way. With large birds on the other hand, such as macaws, the threat lies in the other direction – the kitten's life could be at risk.

Once you have taught your kitten and other animals mutual respect, you should find that you have a happy household!

Teaching Children to Care for a Kitten

A new, small, furry, cuddly little kitten will almost invariably cause a great reaction among the children in your home. They will want to make it the centre of attention, pick it up, play with it, and generally treat it as something akin to a living toy. From the outset, teach your children to handle the kitten gently: it is not a bendy toy, but a little living creature that deserves respect and consideration.

Do allow the kitten time to explore, and discourage children from picking it up frequently. Teach the children the correct way to hold the kitten, so that it feels both secure and content. Never, ever pick up a kitten by the scruff of its neck: hold it by cradling it in your arms, giving support to the front legs, spine and hindquarters. Never let children 'maul' the kitten or squeeze its tummy: if it were to become frightened, it could well lash out and cause blood to be spilled, which is not conducive to helping your kitten settle in happily with your family.

Children and kittens can learn a lot from each other. They both want attention and playtimes, so it is up to you to ensure that this is arranged to the benefit of all parties involved!

Where the Kitten Should Sleep

This is a question that only you can answer, but please bear in mind that once formed, habits die hard. Once you have established night-time accommodation that you think to be suitable, it will be very difficult indeed to persuade your kitten to move.

Most kittens will think it delightful to share your own bed with you and, indeed, many cat owners relish the thought of a small, furry companion as a bed fellow. The advantage to this arrangement is simply that you will rarely need a hot water bottle when winter sets in: cats are wonderfully warm and are quite happy to share their body heat with others! The drawbacks are that they can be restless sleepers, they do tend to shed their fur over everything in sight and love to nibble toes and feet!

If you feel that you do not wish to share your own bed with your cat, then this must be made quite clear from the outset. Find a suitable, warm spot in your house where you feel happy for your kitten to spend its nights. This should be a place that is both warm and draught-free. It should also be a place that your kitten will always regard as its very own bed; this is especially important if there are other pets in the house.

Whatever sleeping arrangements you and your kitten finally agree on, remember that it will be very difficult to change your kitten's habits once it has established its own domain!

CAT AND KITTEN CARE

GROOMING AND WASHING

Cats are most fastidious creatures and spend a large part of their day washing and grooming themselves. However, a little human help does not go amiss, especially if the kitten is of a longhaired variety and you should be prepared to allot some of your time to this most necessary task.

It is important to get your kitten used to a regular grooming programme as soon as possible, paying special attention to the more inaccessible areas, such as under the arms and legs, and the tummy. These are places where the fur is most likely to become knotted. If left unattended for a great length of time, this may necessitate a trip to the vet to have any resulting mats removed under general anaesthetic. An adult cat that has never experienced human grooming, may well put up quite a fight if you try to tease out knots in the more sensitive regions, but if you get a young kitten used to regular brushing and combing, it will accept this as part of the regular routine.

To all cats, grooming plays a much more important function than simply keeping their coats in sparkling condition. Their raspy little tongues remove dead skin and other debris from the fur, as well as stimulating the circulatory system. The latter point is well illustrated in the way that a mother cat will keep washing her newborn kittens: it is not so much that they are dirty, she is simply trying to get their systems going, rather in the way a doctor would shake a newborn baby and slap it on the bottom!

There is also the social aspect of grooming. Cats love to wash each other and it is a sure sign of the acceptance of a new member to your feline family, when mutual grooming is seen to take place! It is not unusual for this to extend to the human owner: it is your kitten's way of saying that it has accepted you as an 'honorary cat'!

It will be necessary to buy special equipment for grooming, and a look around your local pet store will reveal all manner of brushes, combs, claw clippers and feline cosmetics. The types most suitable for your needs depend on the texture and length of your kitten's coat, and it is advisable to choose good-quality products, as they are going to be used frequently. With pale-coated and longhaired varieties, it may even be necessary to give them an occasional bath and, again, if they are accustomed to this while still young, you should have no problems bathing them when they are older.

Where to Groom Your Kitten
A lot of fur will fly around while you are grooming, so, if at all possible, this task should be performed outside. If this is not practical, then the kitchen table or another work surface are both quite suitable. At all times, make sure that the kitten is on a solid surface: a table with wobbly legs is going to make the kitten feel nervous and will not inspire it with confidence for future grooming sessions. Where possible, use a damp, white surface, for one very good reason: you will be able to tell if your kitten has fleas. These nasty little parasites feed on blood and leave their faeces in the kitten's fur. If you find little black specks in your kitten's coat that, when brushed out onto a slightly damp white surface, turn red, that is a sure indication of flea infestation (see page 42).

Mother grooms the kitten, while father looks on

Grooming a Shorthaired Kitten

Equipment Required
A very fine-toothed comb (often called a flea or nit comb), a soft brush, a rubber grooming pad, a chamois leather or piece of velvet and, if the cat is dark-coated, bay rum. For white or pale-coated kittens, shampoo will also be needed and this should be either a special cat shampoo or one designed for babies and small children.

Method
Start with the rubber grooming pad and gently loosen any dead hair and dander (skin debris). Rub the pad both along the line of the fur and against it, as this will give the best result. You will probably find that your kitten loves this, as it also massages its muscles and makes the kitten feel that 'mother' is washing it again. One word of warning: do not overdo this part of grooming as the fur comes out quite easily and you could find that you have a semi-bald kitten.

A lot of dead fur will stay on the pad and can easily be removed with your hand and disposed of. Hand grooming (running the palm of your hand over the cat in a brisk manner) can be most beneficial and, if done while wearing a damp rubber glove, this will remove any dead fur most easily!

Now use the comb, as this will collect up any remaining loose fur. Keep combing until all of this fur has been removed, working from head to tail in the way that the fur naturally lies, but at all times being most careful not to scratch the kitten's skin with the metal teeth. Again, what is collected can easily be pulled off the comb and thrown away.

A soft bristle brush should be used after this, just to ensure that there are no other fine particles left in the fur.

Finally, use the bay rum and the chamois leather or velvet. The bay rum should be splashed on your hands and then rubbed well in to the coat: it will bring out the brilliance of colour in tabbies, torties or any darker-coated cat that should have a sleek coat. For lighter-coated varieties, there are special feline cosmetics that will add that special lustre without darkening the fur. A final polish with a piece of chamois or velvet, and you should now see before you a kitten that positively glows with health, with a coat so shiny that you could almost see your face in it!

Washing a Shorthaired Kitten

On the whole, cats do not like water, but if you have a white or pale-coated cat, the occasional wash may prove necessary. This should be done in a sink or hand basin that can take a shower attachment. Failing this, the bath would suffice but as this is

rather large, it could cause the kitten to panic.

Gently wet the kitten's coat, making sure that all areas have been moistened. Rub the shampoo in well, ensuring that any especially dirty patches are well cleaned, but avoiding the ears, head and eyes. Shower the kitten down with clean water, taking great care that all traces of the shampoo have been removed and that no water or soap goes into ears or eyes. Wrap the kitten up in a clean, warm towel, and give it a good rub down to remove the excess water.

It is most important to dry the kitten off as soon as possible, so that it does not catch a chill, and this can be done in one of two ways. A hairdrier, adjusted to a medium heat setting and held well back from the kitten, is the swiftest method. If you do not own a drier, or if your kitten is frightened by the noise, then wrap it in another clean, warm towel and keep rubbing until the kitten appears dry. Finally warm it in front of a radiator or heater so that it does not catch cold.

After this, the coat will look somewhat fluffy, so rub a little bay rum or other non-greasy conditioner into the fur, followed by a polish with the chamois leather or velvet. This will remove any static, leaving the coat smooth and silky.

Shorthaired kittens will only require grooming about once a week and, once you are used to the methods described, this should only take ten to fifteen minutes. During the moulting season in late spring and early summer, you may find it necessary to groom your kitten more often, but do not overdo it, as the fur is very soft.

Grooming a Longhaired Kitten

Equipment Required
A double-sided, wide, fine-toothed comb, a double-sided wire and bristle brush, a toothbrush, blunt-ended scissors, talcum power, shampoo and conditioner.

Method
Start with the wide-toothed side of the comb, gently separating the hairs and loosening any knotted parts. Be sure to pay great attention to the areas around the legs, tummy and under the tail, as these are most prone to becoming matted. Now use the fine-toothed side, and work through every part of the coat until it is completely free flowing. If there are any serious knots, use the scissors. Cut down through the knot, rather than across it, as this will save as much fur as possible without leaving a bald patch.

Now use the wire side of the brush, which will remove any traces of dead hair from the coat. A sprinkle of talcum powder will add body to the coat, but be most careful not to get this in the kitten's eyes or ears. Brush the excess powder out with the bristle side of the brush.

Finally, use the toothbrush to groom the hair around the face, again being careful to keep this away from the eyes. A last quick run over with the wide side of the comb, flicking the fur forward to show the ruff around the neck, and your kitten should be ready to grace any show bench!

Longhaired kittens should be groomed in this manner at least once a day, and the whole procedure should take about twenty minutes, which is not a great amount of time to spend in order to keep your kitten happy and healthy.

Washing a Longhaired Kitten
Follow the instructions given on page 34 for washing a shorthaired kitten, but, after shampooing and rinsing, apply a good-quality hair conditioner. This can be either a special conditioner made for cats, or a quality product for humans that does not contain perfume. Gently rub the conditioner into the damp coat. If there are any stubborn knotted areas, these

will easily loosen when the conditioner is on the coat, and can then be teased out with the metal comb. When you are happy that the coat is quite free, give a final and thorough rinse, making sure that all traces of shampoo and conditioner are removed.

Wrap the kitten in a warm towel and give it a good rub down to remove surface water. Using a hairdrier and the wide-toothed comb, start to dry the coat off, beginning on the back and gradually working your way to the underneath parts. To start with, you may find that you need to enlist the help of an assistant to hold the drier while you comb the cat. When the fur is almost dry, begin using the bristle end of the brush, as this will fluff the fur up well. Finally, give a sprinkle of talcum powder and another brush up, and your kitten's bathtime is completed.

Regular grooming will not only keep your kitten looking clean and shiny, but has the added benefit of decreasing the chances of fur balls accumulating in the kitten's intestines. These can cause the kitten considerable discomfort (see page 40).

Grooming a shorthaired kitten

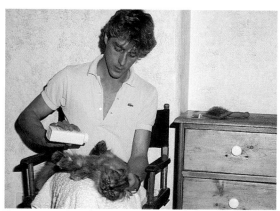

Grooming a Longhair: equipment includes a special wire comb (on dresser) and talcum powder

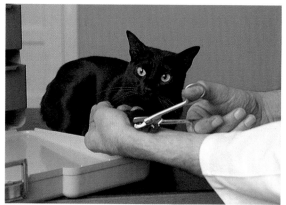

Clipping claws

Care of the Eyes, Ears and Claws

Both eyes and ears will need to be regularly inspected and, if necessary, cleaned. Any unusual discharge from these organs could be an indication of illness and a weekly check will ensure that any infection is nipped in the bud.

Eyes should be gently wiped over with a piece of moistened cotton wool. It is not unusual to find a small deposit of matter in the corner of the eyes, but in all other ways the kitten's eyes should appear bright and clear.

If the nictitating membrane, or haw, is visible, this could be indicative of ill health, and veterinary attention should be sought as soon as possible. Unlike most other animals, cats have three eyelids; two which appear in the same conformation as in the human eye, but the third covering the eye from side to side (see 'haw' in the Glossary).

The ears should also appear clean, with no waxy deposits, and they should not have an unpleasant odour. Inspect the ears weekly and, when necessary, clean them with a little, moistened cotton wool. Never delve deep into the inner ear canal, as this is a delicate organ that can be easily damaged. If your kitten has a dark brown, waxy deposit, a vet should be consulted, as this could be an indication of ear-mite infestation.

Cats keep their claws in trim by scratching and if they do not have access to either a garden or an indoor scratching post, you could well find that your furniture receives a great deal of unwanted attention! It is sometimes necessary to clip a cat's claws and, on the first occasion, it is advisable to get your vet to give you a demonstration of how this should be done correctly. Hold the cat firmly and push the paw pad inwards; the claws will now be unsheathed and visible. Look closely, and you will see that there is a pink area in the middle of each claw, surrounded by a whitish covering which tapers to the sharp end of the claw. The pink area contains the nerves and blood supply, and it would cause pain and bleeding if it were cut into. The white part contains only dead cells, and this is the part of the claw that may be clipped. Special claw clippers can be bought in any pet store, but human nail clippers can be used just as effectively.

INOCULATIONS

Your kitten should be in the peak of health and condition when you first bring it home, and it is your responsibility to ensure that it stays this way. It is not unusual for a kitten to be a bit off colour for a day or so when it is moved to a new home. If it has had to travel any distance, it is quite likely to be somewhat disorientated, and if long-distance, particularly air travel, has been involved, it may even show signs of transport sickness.

Do not worry if it does not want to eat for the first couple of days: kittens, like children, are remarkably resilient and exploring a new domain will most likely take precedence over the thought of food! Equally, all this excitement may cause a 'runny tummy', so do not panic if your kitten's motions are a bit loose at first. If symptoms persist for more than forty-eight hours, however, it would be wise to consult the vet.

'Standard' inoculations

Prevention is always better than cure and your kitten should already have received the necessary inoculations by this time. In the event that these have not been administered, however, contact your vet immediately and arrange for them to be done as soon as possible. In the meantime, do not allow the kitten to mix with other cats, and do not allow it to go outside. Many illnesses can be prevented by inoculation, and these vary from country to country.

FIE

Universally, the most important inoculation is for feline infectious enteritis. This is a viral infection that has a wide area of attack, particularly the bowels and the immune system, and may be compared with canine distemper. The symptoms can be manifold, and may not all appear together. The kitten will seem generally off colour, and will most usually have a hunched apppearance. It will appear depressed, vomit, and suffer from both diarrhoea and dehydration. If your kitten contracts this illness, there is very little hope for recovery.

If you suspect that any symptoms shown could indicate FIE, telephone your vet first just in case he would rather see the kitten at home.

Although the FIE virus is highly contagious between feline hosts, it is easily killed with disinfectants away from the carrier.

An annual 'booster' inoculation will be needed to keep up the immunity to this virus.

Cat 'Flu

This is the common term used to describe two viral infections of the upper respiratory tract, more correctly called FCV (feline calici virus) and FVR (feline viral rhinotracheitis), both of which can appear in either a severe or mild form.

FCV can vary from the kitten being sniffly and sneezy for a few days, to the more serious condition of ulceration of the tongue, mouth and nostrils which will, understandably, cause loss of appetite.

FVR, as the name suggests, is a viral infection which affects, mostly, the nasal area, trachea and lungs.

FCV and FVR may also cause inflammation and a discharge from the eyes, nose and throat, with associated coughing and sneezing as the kitten tries desperately to breathe. The appetite will be affected in severe cases.

Infection by either of these diseases will result in a very pathetic and miserable looking kitten and, if it is not treated immediately by your vet, death may result – the mortality rate for young kittens and, at the other end of the scale, elderly or geriatric cats, is very high.

The viruses on their own will seldom kill but the associated dehydration caused by loss of appetite and fluid loss, in combination with untreated secondary bacterial invasion, frequently results in death.

Recovery in either of these situations may result in the cat becoming a carrier of this virus, which may be shed at times of stress. Both these unpleasant infections are most contagious and, as with FIE, if you suspect that your kitten is displaying these symptoms, ring the vet first before you make a visit to the surgery.

Usually, your kitten will already have received an inoculation before leaving its breeder, and this is normally administered as a three-way vaccine, immunising against FCV, FVR and FIE at the same time. These injections should be given three weeks apart, at either nine and twelve, or twelve and fifteen weeks of age, depending on the vaccine used and your vet's preference.

It is also possible to have the immunisation for 'flu given without an injection, as some brands of vaccine may be administered as a liquid squirted into the nostrils, but these are 'live' vaccines and not suitable in every case.

Rabies

In countries where this killer disease is endemic, it will be necessary to inoculate against it. In some countries this is also a legal requirement, as rabies is one of the few infections that can be transmitted from cats (amongst other animals) to humans. For this reason, those countries that are rabies-free, including Britain, Ireland, Australia, New Zealand and some other islands, impose a quarantine period for all imported animals.

In the UK, rabies inoculations are only given if an animal is being exported to a rabies-infected country. These inoculations can only be administered by a vet who holds a special licence from the Ministry of Agriculture, Fisheries and Food. The rules and regulations vary from time to time, and from country to country, so if you find that you have to move abroad, do consult this ministry, as well as the embassy of the country you are moving to, to make sure that any animals you are taking with you conform to current regulations.

Rabies is also known as hydrophobia as, in the later stages of the disease, the affected animals usually display a tremendous fear of water. Other symptoms can be a change in personality or temperament: a normally quiet cat will become most aggressive, and vice versa. Foaming at the mouth is most common, along with paralysis of the jaws, in the final stages. Once an animal has contracted rabies, there is very little that can be done for it.

If an animal has suspected rabies, the local health authority and police must be informed. The animal's saliva and other bodily discharges will have a very high virus content, and a person with an open wound is just as much at risk as if he or she were actually bitten. The disease is usually transmitted through saliva passed during a bite, but even a lick to an open wound could transmit rabies.

New inoculations

At the time of writing, there are two new breakthroughs in feline immunisation, but these are currently available in the USA only. They are concerned with two infectious diseases, FeLV (feline infectious leukaemia) and FIP (feline infectious peritonitis), both of which, in most circumstances and especially in younger cats and kittens, can result in an extremely high mortality rate. It is to be hoped that these vaccines will soon be available worldwide.

FeLV

This is probably the most currently controversial feline illness and the gutter press is not unknown to refer to it as 'feline AIDS'. The viruses responsible for both FeLV and AIDS are structurally similar and are transmitted in the same way, by prolonged close contact, often of a sexual nature. The FeLV virus cannot exist for long outside a host and is most definitely non-communicable between feline and human: if your kitten has FeLV it *cannot* give you AIDS, and if you have AIDS, there is *no way* that you can infect your kitten with FeLV.

When either you, or your kitten, are ill, it is so very easy to believe that these quite unfounded rumours are true. They are not, so simply ignore them – scaremongering is an easy way to sell a low-quality newspaper!

This said, what are the symptoms of FeLV, and the prognosis if your kitten is affected? Many cats and kittens have a genetically inherited immunity to this disease and even those that do become infected may only be so for a transient period, during which time they build up an acquired immunity.

The symptoms vary a great deal as a cat does not die of FeLV, but of other illnesses associated with the breakdown of immunity to infections. Although, as yet, there is no inoculation for FeLV in the UK, it is possible to have a blood test done on your kitten, which will show whether or not the virus is present in its blood stream. If the test proves positive, a repeat test will be made a fortnight later to confirm that the test is indeed correct, and that the infection is not just a transient type. If the test again proves positive, the prognosis is not good, as, although not unheard of, recovery is rare. A FeLV test is often required on a queen before she is allowed to be mated to a stud.

FIP

This illness seems to affect young cats in particular, and is more rarely seen in cats over three years of age, although it has been known. There are two basic forms of the disease, 'wet' and 'dry', and the symptoms vary accordingly. It is not highly contagious, and is transmitted by direct contact. An infected kitten should, therefore, be isolated from any other cats in the household. The virus cannot live for long outside a feline host.

The classic symptoms of FIP are shown in the wet form, the most noticeable of these being a swelling of the abdomen, as the peritoneal area fills with fluid. This is usually accompanied by signs of general ill health, weight loss, diarrhoea and vomiting.

The dry form is much less obvious, and symptoms appear by way of jaundice, respiratory problems and, as the central nervous system is also attacked in the final stages of the disease, fits.

COMMON AILMENTS

Cats and kittens, on the whole, are pretty healthy little creatures, but there are non-inoculable infections to which they can succumb. As you become used to your kitten and its normal behaviour, you should soon be able to spot when something is amiss. Felines are very much creatures of habit, so any unusual behaviour could be indicative of ill health. Most infections can be cleared up quite easily, but if you have doubts that your diagnosis is correct, or are nervous of treating your kitten yourself, take veterinary advice as soon as possible.

Abscess

An abscess is really like a large pimple, but requires much more careful treatment and, usually, a course of antibiotics. The most common cause of an abscess is a wound suffered during a fight, but one can also develop if a gland becomes infected. It is quite easy to treat an abscess at home, but it is imperative that veterinary advice is sought in order for the appropriate antibiotics to be prescribed.

Gently wash the affected area with a warm saline solution (1 teaspoon of salt in $1/2$ litre boiled, cooled water): this will bring the abscess to a head and the pus can then be gently squeezed out. To prevent the abscess reforming, it will be necessary to keep this up for several days, even a week or more, until all traces of pus have been removed.

Acne

This is most likely to affect a cat or kitten that lives without other feline companions. The chin is the one part of a cat's anatomy that its tongue cannot reach and, unless your kitten has a little friend to help wash this region, it is quite likely that greasy food debris will build up, giving rise to blackheads which can become infected and cause acne. Keep an eye on your kitten's chin and, if necessary, wash it occasionally to keep the area clean.

If your kitten develops this complaint, treat it like an abscess, with a warm compress of saline solution (see Abscess). When the spots come to a head and burst, apply a mild antiseptic, suitable for use on cats, to make sure the infection has gone.

Anal Glands (infection)

On either side of the anal sphincter are two small openings leading to the anal glands, and if these become blocked, this can result in the glands becoming infected. The signs are frequent washing of the anal area, and, as this condition causes considerable irritation, the kitten may also be seen to drag its bottom along the floor to relieve the itchiness. (This is also seen if a kitten is infected with worms – see Parasites.)

Examine the anal area carefully, and you will most likely see two little black specks on either side of the anal opening – these are the blockages. Using some moistened cotton wool, the pus-like contents of the anal glands can be gently squeezed out. Do be careful as, if the glands have become infected, squeezing in the wrong manner can do more harm than good. The contents will smell pretty foul, and if you are a little squeamish, it is best to allow the vet to perform this task! Untreated, anal-gland infection can result in an abscess forming, and this is a most unpleasant affliction to have in such a sensitive area.

Anal Prolapse

This is a condition, sometimes seen in kittens and cats, that is usually the result of constant straining of the rectal muscles due to prolonged problems with either diarrhoea or constipation. A small part of the last section of the bowel will turn inside out, with the result that the kitten will appear to have something looking rather like a raspberry protruding from its anus. This can happen quite suddenly, and veterinary attention should be sought as soon as possible as it may be necessary to correct the prolapse surgically.

It is equally important to correct the cause of the prolapse, and this is most usually done by changing the diet (often to include added bran for roughage) to prevent the condition occuring again.

Arthritis

Although this condition is more likely to affect an older cat, it can, as with humans, develop at any age. Arthritis attacks the joints between bones, causing swelling, inflammation and resulting lameness. Keep the cat warm (a heated pad can be most beneficial and comforting), and allow it plenty of rest. Your vet may prescribe painkillers in severe cases. Obesity can predispose the cat to this condition, as in other species, so for prevention keep your cat at a reasonable weight.

Asthma

As in humans, this is an allergic condition affecting the chest and lungs. Although the exact cause of asthma is not really known, it is most commonly seen in cats in the spring and is attributed to an allergy to pollen. The kitten will show all the symptoms a human would, such as coughing, sneezing, wheezing and general difficulty in breathing.

If your kitten seems to be affected by pollen allergy, the most sensible idea is to keep it indoors, with the windows closed, in springtime, when trees and plants are shedding most of their pollen. Do seek veterinary advice, however, as breathing problems can be symptomatic of a variety of other illnesses.

Constipation

This is something that can affect a cat or kitten at any age, and is usually the result of either an unbalanced diet, or the presence of fur balls (see Fur Balls). The symptoms are straining when the cat tries to pass a motion, hard stools, and sometimes faeces that are spotted with blood as well. The cat will look lethargic, with an 'open' coat, and its haws may be up too.

The administration of liquid paraffin is the most common remedy and this is easily bought over the counter at a chemist's shop or pet store. If the condition does not clear up in a few days, it would be wise to consult a vet, as prolonged constipation can be an indication of more serious illness.

Dandruff

This is seen, as in humans, as whitish, scaly deposits in the fur or hair. All animals shed dead skin from time to time and unless this is regularly removed, it will cause the build up that we refer to as dandruff. The condition is most usually caused by lack of grooming: a good stiff brushing will increase the circulation, aiding healthy skin and fur growth, and will normally clear up the problem. If the dandruff persists, it may be necessary to consult a vet who will probably prescribe a special shampoo.

Diabetes

Diabetes may affect a cat at any age, but it is usually a condition associated with obesity and older age. An affected cat will display classic symptoms of increased thirst and appetite, but with accompanied, unexpected weight loss. It will be necessary for a vet to make tests on blood and urine samples to confirm the condition.

Treatment is a daily insulin injection which, once you have been given a demonstration by your vet, you can administer yourself. It is equally important to give meals at regular times, and to ensure that any foods containing carbohydrates or sugar are removed from the diet. Once the correct diagnosis has been made, there is no reason why a diabetic kitten or cat cannot live to a ripe old age, as long as the correct medication and diet are provided.

Diarrhoea

Loose motions are a very common occurrence in a kitten, and should not be the cause of too much worry unless they persist for more than two or three days. Kittens have sensitive little tummies, and the delicate bacterial balance in the intestines, which aids the digestion of food, can easily be upset.

If your kitten has diarrhoea, keep it off solid foods, let it drink as much *still* mineral (not tap) water as it likes, and give it a teaspoon of *live* yoghurt three times a day. Live yoghurt contains natural bacteria that will help to restore the natural balance in the intestines, and it is a harmless but effective treatment for a 'runny tum'! If there is no improvement in forty-eight hours, or the condition worsens, seek veterinary advice.

Dilated Pupil Syndrome: *see Feline Dysautonomia*

Eczema

Eczema can be caused in many ways – the main problem being that it will still look the same, thus making diagnosis of the cause, and subsequent treatment, difficult! It can be hereditary, in which case it is often linked with asthma, as it is in humans.

Hormone imbalance, usually caused by a female kitten being spayed too early, can give rise to a condition known as miliary eczema. (Other factors can also give rise to this condition, but experts believe that the most common cause is a flea allergy.) Miliary eczema caused by too-early spaying will need to be treated with a regular course of hormone replacement.

Eczema is often caused by a bad diet, which is easily rectified by changing the food. However, it can also be caused by an allergy to fleas or other parasites, and any hair loss and/or scaly patches should receive veterinary attention very soon.

Feline Dysautonomia (*previously known as Key-Gaskell Syndrome or the Dilated Pupil Syndrome*)

This condition has only been seen in recent years, and was first described by Key and Gaskell of the Veterinary Department of Bristol University in England.

The most usual symptom of this syndrome is that an affected cat will show permanently dilated pupils. Hence the previous terms used. Most often, both eyes will show this dilation, but in some cases only one eye is affected and, much more rarely, the eyes can even appear normal. Other symptoms include dryness of the nose and mouth, difficulty in eating and swallowing, constipation, vomiting and gagging.

Although it has been known to affect cats as old as eleven years old, it seems to be more common in kittens and young cats. At present, it is not known how the disease is transmitted, nor how contagious it is, but research is continuing. It is difficult to diagnose and this diagnosis can only be made by a veterinary surgeon. The cause is unknown and treatment is symptomatic. The mortality rate is high; a recent figure showed that nearly 75 per cent of affected cats die.

Feline Infectious Anaemia (FIA)

FIA is a protozoan infection that is thought to be transmitted by fleas and mosquitoes. For some, as yet unknown reason, FIA seems to affect young male cats far more often than females. The symptoms are general lethargy and lack of appetite, while, typically, the lips, gums and mouth will lose their healthy pink colour and appear pale.

The disease can be detected by microscopic analysis of a blood sample, and if this proves positive for FIA, the vet will most likely do another test for FeLV, as FIA often develops as a side effect of this infectious leukaemia virus. Simple FIA infection is treatable, if caught in the early stages, but if combined with FeLV, the prognosis is not so hopeful.

Fits

Fits are not often seen in kittens, but if your kitten has one, seek veterinary advice as soon as possible. The most usual reason for fits is one of several viral infections, or toxic poisoning, and the true cause should be diagnosed and treated without delay.

Fur Balls

When a cat or kitten grooms itself, a certain amount of loose hair will be removed and swallowed. Fur is indigestible, and, if a lot of fur is taken into the intestine, a blockage may well occur, which is commonly referred to as a fur ball. This is most usually treated by the administration of one teaspoonful of liquid paraffin twice a day for three days in an adult cat, and less for kittens. However, the condition is easily prevented by regular grooming of the cat by its owner – this is especially important with longhaired varieties.

Haematoma

This is a swelling, looking not unlike an abscess, but filled with blood. It is usually the result of constant scratching, a blow, or a bite, and is commonly seen on the ear. It is important to get this treated by a vet as soon as possible: the ear is a delicate organ, and if this condition is not treated promptly, it will result in the kitten having a 'flop' ear for life.

Key-Gaskell Syndrome: *see Feline Dysautonomia*

Mouth and Teeth Problems

In kittens, the most common 'disorder' is teething, but it is another point that few people remember! The first teeth will start to come through at about five to six weeks old, and usually cause no problems. However, at around sixteen to eighteen weeks, the adult teeth begin to appear and these can cause a certain amount of soreness and discomfort in the kitten.

Unlike in a human, a kitten's teeth do not fall out before another lot come down; the adult teeth do, in fact, push the first lot out! This is fine 90 per cent of the time, but occasionally they 'misfire'. You then have a situation where two teeth appear side by side. This causes swelling and discomfort and often makes a kitten go off its food and cause its haws to appear.

If the milk teeth do not come out naturally, it is sometimes necessary to consult a vet, who will be able to prescribe a soothing balm, but *never* use a preparation manufactured for a human child.

Mainly, it will be in middle to old age that teeth problems arise. With the advent of tinned cat food, which, although it provides a good, balanced diet, tends to be rather soggy, cats are increasingly prone to tooth decay and gum disease. In the wild, cats would catch mice and birds and devour them bones and all. Few domestic cats do this nowadays, and so it is important to give your cat something to chew on to restore the natural balance. Chomping away on a bone keeps the jaws active, the gums well massaged, and the teeth free from tartar.

However, you must never give your cat chicken or rabbit bones, although a cooked beef knuckle bone is most beneficial. The occasional small handful of crunchy cat biscuits, pork scratchings or any other crunchy food, will help to keep your cat's teeth healthy.

If the teeth are causing distress, the cat will most likely try to scratch at its mouth. Take the cat to a vet, as it is likely that the teeth will have to be surgically cleaned, or perhaps even an extraction may be necessary. In these days of modern science, teeth can be cleaned very quickly and effectively with specialised veterinary equipment.

Mouth problems can also occur when a foreign body becomes lodged in the mouth or throat. The signs are quite similar to teeth problems; the cat will try to scratch, or even tear, at the affected area, so do make sure that you summon veterinary advice as soon as possible.

Ringworm

This is really a misnomer, as it is a fungal infection that affects the fur and skin, and has no known connection with worms! It is a very contagious condition, and correct diagnosis should be made as soon as possible in order that the, albeit lengthy, treatment can be begun.

Unfortunately, the symptoms can vary, which makes diagnosis difficult, but any hair loss should be treated as suspect. Most forms of ringworm will fluoresce when viewed under a special ultra-violet light, known as a Wood's lamp. This test should be carried out in a darkened room, so do not be surprised if your vet closes the blinds and turns off the room lights when examining your kitten!

Treatment for ringworm is simple, bur prolonged, and will require an antibiotic called griseofulvin to be administered on a regular basis for up to a month or more. It may also be necessary to use a fungicidal shampoo as well.

With longhaired breeds, it may be necessary to clip the coat in order to expedite treatment. The antibiotic works by getting into the bloodstream and killing the fungus as the new fur grows – the longer the fur, the longer it will take for the antibiotic to work.

An infected cat should be isolated, and a regime of strict hygiene must be employed – all bedding should be burned and replaced with new, following your vet's advice for laundering.

Ringworm is another of the very few conditions that can be transferred from feline to human, so you should keep an eye out for any itchy, scaly patches developing on you or your family – if they do, the treatment is just the same, only it will be your doctor who prescribes the griseofulvin!

After a month to six weeks, your vet will wish to examine the kitten under the Wood's lamp again, just to ensure that the infection has completely cleared and that no fluorescing particles remain: at this point, you and your household can return to normal!

PARASITES

Internal Parasites

Worms

The most common internal parasites found in cats and kittens are roundworms and tapeworms, and both can be cleared by a course of worming treatment. Roundworms can cause serious loss of condition in a young kitten, resulting in diarrhoea or constipation, anaemia and a pot-bellied appearance.

These worms live in the intestine and feed on the

partly digested food the kitten has eaten. When the worms breed, their eggs pass out in the kitten's faeces, and other cats sharing the same litter tray are likely to become infected.

Tapeworm infection is not so serious, mostly causing irritation in the affected kitten, but it should be treated just the same. The most obvious sign of tapeworm infestation is the presence of what look like white grains of rice around the anal region, which are the tapeworms eggs. Tapeworms need an intermediate host to continue their life cycle, and this is most usually a flea, so it is important to treat the kitten for fleas as well.

It is best to ask your vet to recommend suitable worming preparations: there are some that treat both roundworms and tapeworms in one pill, whereas others act only on one type of worm, not both. In any event, read the instructions very carefully, and ensure that you give exactly the correct dose.

Toxoplasmosis
Although not specifically a parasitic infection, it is appropriate to mention toxoplasmosis at this point. This is a coccidial disease endemic in many countries. It is a zoonosis, a disease communicable between humans and animals, and this disease is particularly associated with the cat family.

Toxoplasmosis rarely causes symptoms or illness in the cat itself. Its importance lies mostly in the fact that the faeces of symptomless carriers often contain large amounts of infective cysts: these cysts are so small that they cannot be seen and can only be detected by laboratory tests. Toxoplasmosis rarely causes disease in humans, but constitutes a real danger to pregnant women and the human foetus. For this reason pregnant women should be advised to handle cats as little as possible. They should be particularly careful to wash their hands after handling cats and should delegate litter-changing to others. Boiling water kills the cysts and this should be used routinely to sterilise litter trays, feeding containers and grooming equipment.

External Parasites
Fleas, ticks and mites are all external parasites that your kitten may succumb to at some stage in its life, especially if it has access to the outside world, where it will meet up with strange cats and other animals.

Fleas
Fleas are the most common parasite your cat is likely to pick up, especially during the spring and summer months when the weather is warmer and the flea population is on the increase. Fleas feed by sucking the blood from a feline host, and as this causes considerable irritation, the first sign of flea infestation

is that your kitten will scratch itself frequently, particularly around the head and the back of the neck.

Close examination of the coat will most likely show little specks of what look like black grit: these are the flea droppings, and confirm the suspicion that fleas are present. Your kitten should be treated immediately and, in the first instance, it is best to consult your vet who will prescribe the most suitable preparation. Flea sprays and powders bought over the counter from a pet shop are not always the most efficacious, and, as some are dangerous to very young kittens, it is best to let your vet make the decision as to treatment.

It is possible to buy flea collars for cats, which are impregnated with a flea killer, but they are not tremendously effective and, in some kittens, can cause an allergic reaction on contact with the skin, giving rise to a form of dermatitis.

Some cats are allergic to the actual flea bite, and nasty weals and sores can result in such cases. Also, fleas are the intermediate hosts to tapeworms and, if untreated, your kitten may become a host to this internal parasite as well.

Regular spraying of your kitten and its bedding, during the warmer months, should keep your kitten's coat free of parasites, and regular grooming with a fine-toothed flea comb will help also.

Ticks
Ticks are also blood suckers but, unlike the flea who hops from host to host, these nasty little parasites bury their heads deep in the cat's skin, remaining there until they are physically removed. The tick sucks the cat's blood, its body swelling up as a fat, grey pea-sized balloon.

It is quite easy to remove it yourself: a tick's head has hooks that attach it to its host and these can be anaesthetised with surgical alcohol. (Gin or vodka work just as well, but are rather an expensive way to rid your kitten of this problem!) Swab the tick with the alcohol and, with a pair of tweezers, pull if off. It is most important to make sure the whole tick has been removed, as, if the head is left behind, infection will set in, resulting in an abscess. If this all sounds a bit gruesome, then it is best left to your vet! Ticks are rarely found in urban cats, as they are most usually acquired in pasture used to graze sheep and cattle. If you live in the country, you should inspect your kitten's coat regularly for any sign of ticks.

Mites
There are two main types of mites that may take up residence on a cat. These are fur (or skin) mites and ear mites. Mites that attack the fur will cause

the condition known as mange, resulting in fur loss and a scaly, scabby condition in the skin. This will normally be seen around the head and facial area, but as it can look like ringworm, it is best to take the kitten to a vet for a confirmed diagnosis and treatment.

Ear-mite infestation is hard to mistake. It causes a thick, brown, waxy build-up in the ear canal, which gives off a most distinct and unpleasant smell. This must be dealt with by your vet, who will clear out the ears as much as possible and then administer a course of ear drops. You should be very careful about cleaning the ear canal yourself: the ear is a very delicate organ and can easily be damaged by an inexperienced hand.

ACCIDENTS AND FIRST AID

Although it is possible that your kitten may suffer from some of the above-mentioned infections, it is far more likely that your visits to the vet will be because of accidents. Kittens are much more 'elastic' and athletic than puppies, which are unable to jump up onto a surface much higher than a sofa or chair, and so rarely get themselves into a situation that they cannot get out of!

The complete reverse is true of kittens: they can, and will, get into everything and anything, unless you exert the utmost vigilance! Their natural curiosity can cause them to end up in the most precarious situations, sometimes resulting in tragic consequences, so the remainder of this section is given over to the sort of accidents that can occur, and how to administer emergency first aid if the worst does happen. With any accident or injury, *shock*, whether immediate or delayed, can be more of a problem than the injury or accident itself.

Abrasions, Cuts and Wounds
The treatment for these depends very much on the severity of the wound.

A small skin abrasion, where only the surface of the skin has been broken, can easily be treated at home. Gently bathe the affected area with a piece of cotton wool soaked in diluted antiseptic, to prevent infection. A little lanolin-based antiseptic cream can then be applied, which will speed the healing of the wound and the regrowth of fur. The treatment should be applied daily until the abrasion has healed.

Long, deep and bleeding wounds will require veterinary attention as soon as possible and, unless it is unavoidable, should be left well alone until professional advice can be sought. If this is not possible, you can help by administering first aid immediately, until the vet is present.

Again bathe the area with diluted antiseptic, and then apply a pressure bandage to try to stem the bleeding: this should be an absorbent pad that will cover the wound, which is then held in place with an evenly wound bandage.

Untrained hands should never attempt to apply a tourniquet. With the best of intentions, you could cause even more severe problems in the affected limb by completely stopping the blood flow, which could result, in the worst cases, in amputation. It is much safer merely to put a cold compress over the pressure bandage, as this will stem the bleeding in the immediate area of the wound, without risking damage to the rest of the limb.

Bites
Bites, especially from other cats, are probably the most common form of wound that your kitten will encounter, especially if it is allowed free range. Fighting for territorial rights is second nature to felines, and their disagreements can result in quite nasty bites. For any bite, whatever the size, treat the wound immediately with diluted antiseptic or saline solution, and 'phone the vet at once. Even a small puncture wound could develop into an abscess, and it is imperative that an antibiotic injection is administered as soon as possible, followed up with a course of antibiotic pills.

The mouth of any animal (including that of a human) contains all sorts of bacteria that can get into the blood stream and cause severe infection, so the antibiotic course is all important. Whenever you find a bite or scratch, always cut the hair over and around the area: this aids healing and helps you find the place again more easily for further treatment. (For other bites, see *Stings and Bites*.)

Burns and Scalds
These are most likely to arise when your kitten enters an unattended kitchen where warmth from the oven and the interesting smells from a boiling pan will be irresistible to a nosey cat.

A burn is caused when the skin is in direct contact with a hot surface; a scald is the result of hot fluids touching the skin. Both will cause blisters to form, and the treatment is the same.

Wherever possible, the vet should be contacted at once. If there is any delay, apply *only* a soothing cold pad. Do *not* put any ointments or lotions on the burn, and take the cat to a vet immediately.

Burns can also be the result of contact with caustic materials, such as acids. A caustic burn will look the same as any other burn, with the same associated blistering. However, the kitten may well have ingested the caustic substance as well, and this will require immediate attention. An emetic should be administered immediately and this is most easily produced from the kitchen cupboard in the form of salt mixed with water.

Drowning
Although cats are commonly known to hate water, they can get themselves into all sorts of situations that may result in drowning. For a cat that does not go outside, drowning could occur through contact with a variety of domestic appliances: washing machines, baths and toilets being the main causes.

For cats that are allowed outside, there are the added dangers of tanks, ponds, lakes and swimming pools.

In the case of a nearly drowned cat that does not appear to be breathing, *immediate* emergency first aid must be administered. Hold the hind limbs firmly and swing the cat back and forth in order to remove any water from the lungs: continue until the cat begins to show signs of life.

If the cat is not breathing it will also be necessary to give mouth-to-mouth resuscitation, and this is performed in very much the same manner as recommended by the Red Cross, and other such organisations, for human resuscitation – only it is better to breathe into the cat's nose rather than its mouth. Tilt the cat's head back, hold the mouth shut with your fingers and breathe heavily into both nostrils: wait a few seconds until the air is expelled, and continue. Once the cat is breathing on its own, it will not be necessary to continue this procedure.

If the affected cat still appears not to be breathing, it will be necessary to massage the heart in order to get this all important organ pumping again. If the heart is still not working after that, then to all intents and purposes the cat is dead – but it may even still be possible to revive it, albeit by drastic measures! Lie the cat on its side and rapidly press and release the area of the chest behind the elbow, where the heart lies. This is the only way that you will get the heart going again.

As the cat is theoretically dead, it will not feel what is going on, so if you do happen to misjudge the strength of your action, what is a broken rib compared to saving a life?

Contact your vet immediately, and he or she will give you further instructions and advice. To prevent such accidents, keep the toilet lid down, cover the swimming pool and keep a close eye on the contents of your washing machine before you switch it on.

Electric Shock
Wires and cables are easy to chew through and it is best to educate your kitten as to these dangers. If your kitten does suffer from an electric shock, keep it warm and restrained, with its head pointing upwards. Resuscitation should be administered in the ways described for drowning.

Falls
Cats have the most incredible flexibility and, when falling, nearly always seem to land on all four paws without causing any damage to themselves. If a cat falls from a great height, the major danger it may sustain is a head injury, which will most likely lead to concussion. If this is the case, take the cat to a vet as soon as possible.

Even if the cat appears to be all right, there is always the possibility of internal injuries, such as a bruised liver or spleen so, again, it would be wise to take the cat to a vet for a thorough checkover.

Shock can easily set in, so do make sure your cat is warm (but not too warm and certainly not hot) and quiet whilst you contact the vet.

Poison
Cats, possibly more than any other animals, are most susceptible to poisoning and can succumb, and react, to toxins in a variety of ways.
1 The most common cause of poisoning is by the human hand. Some people think that if their cat is 'off-colour', aspirin and codeine may make it feel better, but many 'human' drugs are extremely poisonous to felines. Equally dangerous are such common items as slug killers and many commonly used garden pesticides.
2 Disinfectants that contain cresols or phenols are equally dangerous; they may be quite safe to use with humans or dogs, but will cause great distress to a cat.
3 Foreign vapours, such as those given off by solvents, paint, glue, varnish, etc., weigh more than air and are therefore more concentrated at floor level than in the upper areas of a room. Cats are most susceptible to inhaling these fumes, and can be poisoned by them. Most often, the signs of inhaled poison will be difficulty in breathing, accompanied by swelling of the trachea or wind pipe.
4 Cats can absorb poison in many ways and their skin and paw pads are particularly susceptible. So do be careful when preparing an outside run and make sure you use Cuprinol, which is safe when dry, and not creosote. Many forms of detergent can also poison cats, even by just getting on their coats.

By whatever means your cat has been poisoned, you must act quickly and contact a vet at once. If the cat has taken poison by mouth, you can try to make it sick by administering an emetic, such

Retrieving a young Burmese

as salted water. If you know what the poison is, keep some to show to the vet, or, if your cat has been sick, keep this so that an analysis can be made if necessary. Using this information, a vet should be able to treat a cat as quickly as possible. In the meantime if you have some natural yoghurt, or powdered charcoal, try to get your cat to swallow some, as this can act as a neutraliser.

Road Accidents

Motor vehicles are responsible for the deaths of more cats and kittens than any other single factor, and it is wise to keep your kitten away from roads as much as possible.

If your cat has been involved in such an accident, but has managed to stagger home, wrap it in a towel, keep it warm and rush it to the vet.

If a cat or kitten is found in the road, either unconscious or unable to move, be very careful in lifting it, as further damage could be caused by bad handling. Using a blanket as a stretcher, gently lift the cat up, being most careful to keep it in the same position as it was found – do not let the head dangle downwards, but keep it well supported and slightly lower than the body to allow blood to reach the brain. This is important if the cat is in shock.

Unless absolutely necessary, do not give first aid, but in the event that you cannot get to a vet very quickly, try the following first aid procedures. With any open and bleeding wound, apply a pressure bandage as described earlier. If no such material is available, use your hand to put pressure on the wound to curtail the bleeding. Keep the cat warm and reassured. Stroke it gently and speak to it quietly until you can get veterinary assistance.

Snake Bites

It is most important to act quickly if your cat has been bitten by a snake, as the venom will spread through the cat's blood system at great speed. If you are unable to get to a vet within a short time, it will be necessary to apply a tourniquet to prevent the spread of the venom. This really is a last resort, and should not be attempted by unpractised hands, but in a life or death situation it is better than doing nothing at all (you would need a more detailed reference book for instructions).

Your first action, however, should be to ring the nearest vet and ask who stocks an anti-serum for the particular snake in question, and then get your cat there as fast as possible.

In the UK the only venomous snake is the adder.

Stings

It is quite likely that at some point in your cat's life it will be stung by an insect, such as a bee or wasp.

In the spring and summer, when such flying insects are most active, it is possible that your cat will try to catch one and then attempt to eat it. This can be dangerous as a sting will cause considerable swelling which, if it occurs in the throat, will result in constriction of the trachea, thus leading to difficulty in breathing. Emergency procedure is then necessary. Put a small ice cube inside its mouth and place a small pack of frozen peas or the like on its throat to stop the swelling, and get the cat to a vet, fast.

Bee stings, unlike wasp stings which only cause inflammation, have to be removed as they can cause a toxic reaction. This is because bees actually leave their stings embedded in their victims, whereas wasps do not. In either case, if your cat is stung in the mouth or throat it is important to let the vet examine it as soon as possible.

In the autumn, it is more likely that your cat will be stung on a paw: at this time of year both bees and wasps are very drowsy, so it is possible that the cat may inadvertently step on one, or play with a sleepy one, and so get stung.

Wasp stings are not as worrying as bee stings and a soothing cold compress or dunking the part in a bowl of cold water will alleviate the inflammation.

GENERAL EMERGENCY ADVICE

What to Do if Your Kitten goes Missing

If your kitten appears to be missing there are several things you can do to try to find it. This is more likely to be a problem if the kitten is allowed into the garden, or is afforded a free-range lifestyle, than with a cat that is confined indoors, or to an escape-proof cat run. However, even in the latter two situations, it may happen that your kitten could get out, especially in the summer months when windows are often left open. You would be surprised at just how small a space a cat will manage to crawl through! The best way to locate a missing feline is to take the following course of action, and not panic!

1 Check your house thoroughly to make sure that the cat really is missing – it is a pointless exercise to go out on a cold night searching the streets, only to discover that the 'missing' cat had managed to get locked in the bathroom! (I know, I've done it and my neighbours must have thought me completely mad!) Pay special attention to warm spots in the house, such as the airing cupboard, and behind the refrigerator and television.

Check all cupboards and drawers (one of my cats managed to spend a peaceful night locked in the bottom drawer of my desk – it was only when she did not appear for breakfast that I realised something was afoot, and then heard a plaintive miaow coming from that part of the room. She was not hurt, but to show her disgust at my carelessness she ate all the files stored in that drawer and refused to talk to me for a week; cats have a wonderfully subtle way of making you feel guilty!) If there is still no sign, then start to look further afield.

2 Think of any possible 'escape' points, and search the area immediately outside, e.g. if you find that the kitchen window has been left ajar, search that part of the garden first, calling the cat's name. Toilet and bathroom windows seem to be regular escape routes for the adventurous kitten, as these are often inadvertently left open.

3 Ask your neighbours to look in their garages, gardens and sheds, and in their own houses – make sure to tell them the sort of places that a cat may hide in, as listed in 1. Be sure to give a good description of the cat. Most people do not know what the different breeds look like, so do not just say, 'Seal Colourpoint Persian', but describe the cat fully, such as 'a longhaired cat with pale cream fur, dark brown face, ears, tail and legs, and with large blue eyes'. Even better, show them a photograph and, if you have another cat that looks the same, show them that too.

4 If nothing transpires within a few hours, begin to notify the following:
a) The RSPCA, PDSA, Petwatch and all the cat rescue groups in your area (you will find these listed in your local telephone directory).
b) All the local veterinary surgeons (if the cat has been injured it is quite likely that some kind soul will take it to a vet)
c) If it is a pedigree cat, contact the breeder – most cat breed clubs have a 'lost and found' service and the breeder should be able to put you in contact with them.
d) The police: although they are really not interested in cats, you may find that the duty officer is sympathetic. If it is a pedigree cat, make sure that you mention this fact and that it is a 'valuable' animal, as the reason it is missing could possibly be theft.
e) The milkman, postman and newspaper boy or girl: cats that are not used to being outside will quickly revert to their natural instincts and only come out under cover of darkness. People who are out in the streets early in the morning are more likely to see your missing cat.

5 Make up some notices to put on trees and lampposts in the neighbourhood. Give a good description of the cat, using a photograph if possible, but in this instance do not mention that the cat is of any financial value, merely a much-loved family pet. The offer of a reward may well encourage people to be vigilant!

6 This is a nasty one, but I always feel that it is better to know than not – your Local Borough Cleansing Department. If the cat has been run over, they are most likely to have found the body. You may prefer to get a friend to handle this one for you, as it is obviously distressing.

If none of these bring any result, do not give up hope: your cat may even have got into a car and been transported quite some distance, and it will take time before this is realised. It is not unknown for cat and owner to be reunited weeks, sometimes, months, later. If you have moved house, do go back to your original home, as a cat will often try to return to its original environment.

It is interesting to note that quite often, even after a period of about three days, a cat or kitten will be found only yards away from the point at which it was originally lost: they do not often wander far.

Lastly, there is something that few people think of but it is certainly a point to consider! Some cats do respond to their owners' voices, but food is usually the best reason for a cat to want to come back home. Think about making a noise, such as ringing a bell, just before you feed your cat each day. Just like Pavlov's dogs, your cat will soon begin to associate that sound with food. If it wanders off, it will soon come running to the sound of the special noise and the thought of a meal. My own cats come to the sound of a bikkies box being rattled – if I am unsure of their whereabouts, the sound of those rattling bikkies brings them all out of their hiding places in no time at all!

How to Take Your Kitten's Temperature
The first point to make is that, unless you already have some useful veterinary experience, it is not advisable to attempt to use a thermometer on a cat. Until recently, thermometers have been available only in the form of mercury encased in a glass tube. Such a device should not be used by a novice, as the glass could break, with tragic results. However, a plastic thermometer is now available with a digital read-out, which is much easier to use.

The temperature of a cat is taken in the rectum and any device inserted into this delicate area should be used very carefully as it is easy to damage the delicate structure of the rectum. Even when using a plastic thermometer, make sure that the cat is well restrained; if you are not sure that you can keep the cat still, it is best not even to try to take its temperature. The normal temperature of a healthy cat is 38.6°C (101.5°F).

Taking a cat's temperature

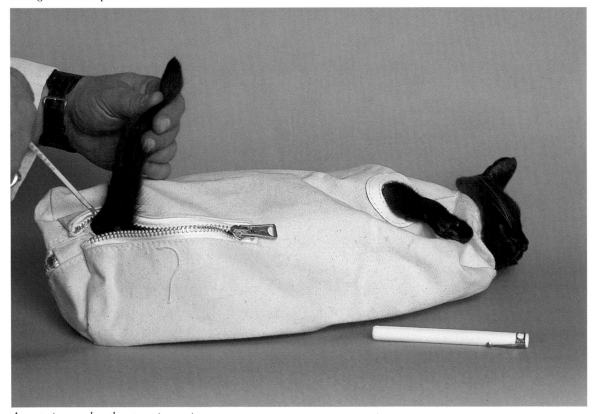

A restrainer makes the operation easier

The easiest way to tell if your cat or kitten has a high temperature is to feel its ears. A cat's ears should feel considerably cooler than the rest of its body, so if they seem to be abnormally warm, this is indicative of a change in body temperature.

How to Administer Pills

If your kitten is ill, it is most probable that your vet will ask you to administer a course of pills or tablets. This is not difficult, and can be done in one of two ways. First is the do-it-yourself method. This is usually the easiest way of pill-popping your cat as long as it trusts you.

Place your hand over the cat's jaw, with thumb and middle finger on either side. Push, and you will find that the cat's mouth opens, shoot the pill to the back of the throat, and close the mouth at once – you will be surprised how quickly and easily this can be done!

Alternatively, you could buy a 'pill giver', which is a long device that will enable a pill to be 'shot' down the cat's throat without any problems.

After giving a pill, do watch to make sure the cat does not spit it out of the side of its mouth.

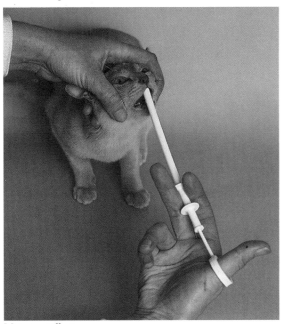

Using a pill giver

General Advice on Caring for a Sick Kitten

Whatever problem your kitten is suffering from, be it caused through illness or accident, basic care is the same. Keep it warm and comfortable, and, if it has an infectious disease, away from other animals.

Using sensible household hygienic precautions, you should find that your kitten will bounce back into full health in no time at all.

Lastly

Many human drugs can be most harmful to felines. *Never* give a human drug to a cat without consulting your vet. The following list shows those common drugs that should *never* be administered to a cat:

Aspirin
Panadol
Codeine
Kaolin and morphine

FEEDING YOUR KITTEN

A correct and balanced diet is all important if your kitten is to develop into a healthy adult cat. If you have bought a pedigree kitten direct from a breeder, or taken in a rescued kitten from a cat sanctuary, you should find that you have been supplied with a diet sheet. This will list the type of food the kitten is used to, size of portions and the frequency of mealtimes. It will also explain how the diet should change as the kitten grows older. Follow the diet sheet carefully, but if you are at all worried, the breeder will not mind if you ask for advice on any dietary problems.

If, unwisely, you have bought your kitten from a pet shop, it is unlikely that you will be given this sort of information – in all probablility you will, instead, have been persuaded to buy several tins of the most expensive brand of cat food!

Feeding from Three to Nine Months Old

When you first bring your kitten home, it should be about twelve weeks old. It is quite likely that your new kitten may not want to eat for the first day or so, but this is no reason for panic. Moving home is a major upheaval for anyone, not least of all a small kitten, and this is quite likely the cause of the loss of appetite!

Kittens have very small stomachs, but still need as much, if not more food than an adult cat. For this reason they need to be fed small quantities of food, but at more frequent mealtimes. Between three and six months old, your kitten will require four meals a day: a good breakfast and afternoon meal, with a lighter lunch and supper. At this age, the portion sizes should be approximately one heaped tablespoon per kitten per larger meal.

At six months, the midday meal can be dropped and the portion sizes increased accordingly. As the kitten approaches adulthood, at nine months old, the evening meal may be dispensed with as well. At this age you are feeding your kitten as you would an adult cat, and the two daily meals should contain roughly two heaped tablespoons of food each (about half a small tin of cat food) per meal. This amount should be quite adequate.

Adapting to solid food

What to Feed Your Kitten

'A little of what you fancy does you good' is a fine motto for feeding your kitten, but with a few reservations!

Proprietary brands of tinned cat food are sold as complete meals, and comprise a specially prepared, balanced diet containing all the vitamins and minerals that your cat needs. For younger kittens, a special tinned kitten food is also available, and this has been specially designed to balance nutritional requirements with the small size of a kitten's stomach, thus giving your kitten the best possible diet during its months of development.

Tinned pilchards and sardines are usually well received, but should not be given too frequently to younger kittens, as they are rather rich and could cause a tummy upset. It is better to wait until your kitten is over six months old before feeding it these types of fish.

Dry and semi-moist cat foods are also available, but it is better to give these as an occasional treat rather than as a complete meal. Try sprinkling a little dry food on the main meal, as this will give your kitten something to exercise its jaws on, and help to keep its teeth in good condition. The low water content of these foods can cause bladder and kidney problems in some cats in later life, so they should be used sparingly and only when there is a plentiful supply of fresh water available for the kitten.

A final type of new feline convenience food is fresh fish, meat or chicken, that has been vacuum packed in small punnets, and contains no preservatives or colourings at all, thus making it exceptionally suitable for a kitten. At present, however, this is available only in the UK and Europe.

Your kitten will love a meal of fresh food and, if possible, at least one meal a day should be specially prepared and cooked. Always buy fresh food that is suitable for human consumption: meat 'for animal consumption only' can, in fact, cause a tummy upset. Equally, 'pet mince', bought from a butcher or pet store, often has a high fat content, and this is not good for a kitten.

Most fresh foods are suitable for a kitten; such as white fish (make sure that the skin and *all* bones have been removed), flaked or cut into small pieces; lean beef and veal, minced or cut into small pieces; chicken and rabbit that have been *very* carefully boned and finely chopped or minced (ensure that even the tiny splintery bones are removed, as these can lodge in the throat, just like fish bones); offal, such as kidney and heart, chopped or cut into small pieces; scrambled egg (not too often); or a slice of the Sunday roast, chopped, with a little gravy added.

Pork and lamb may be given occasionally, but as they are more fatty meats, not too often. A little fat *is* needed in the diet, but too much can cause digestive problems in a kitten. Liver is very rich in vitamin A, and so should not be given to kittens, or older cats, nor, in any circumstances, should it form the basic part of the cat's diet. It does, however, cause an interesting, and sometimes useful, reaction in cats: raw liver loosens the bowels, and so can help relieve constipation, whilst cooked liver has the opposite effect and can help to firm up the motions of a cat with diarrhoea.

Cow's milk is not a suitable food: it is designed to feed calves, not kittens, and can often cause diarrhoea in the latter. It is much better to use a little evaporated milk diluted with water, or powdered milk manufactured for human babies, if your kitten or cat likes milky foods. At *all times* fresh water must be available to your kitten.

Raw, fresh red meat may be offered to your kitten if you wish, but any such raw food must be absolutely fresh, and of a quality fit for human consumption. Not all cats like raw meat (do you?), but it will do no harm if this is a preference. The most suitable meats to give uncooked are beef or horse. Never feed uncooked poultry, fish or pork.

Equally, you may like to give your kitten a cooked bone occasionally; this will keep the teeth and gums strong and healthy. Chicken and rabbit bones should not be given, but a chop bone from lamb or pork can be most beneficial and, if you can stand the mess that will ensue, most kittens and cats will be more than happy to polish off the remains of the Sunday joint – but always put such foods in the cat's own special feeding area, and do not allow it to steal from the table.

When feeding fresh food, it is advisable to add some extra vitamins and supplements to the meal. A liquid preparation containing multi-vitamins, of the type designed for human babies, can be purchased and this is just as beneficial to feline ones. A single drop in each meal will ensure that your growing kitten has all the vitamins it needs!

Powders which contain all the minerals and trace elements that a kitten needs can also be bought at pet stores. These have a high level of calcium and will help to promote the growth of strong, healthy bones.

While tinned cat foods have been specially balanced for your kitten, fresh foods are not, so the addition of a little roughage is important: a little natural bran, cereal, wholemeal brown bread, corn flakes or muesli should be added to any fresh-food meal, to aid digestion and help the easy passage of stools.

Lastly, always give your kitten its food at room temperature. If you keep an open tin of cat food in the refrigerator, put the amount required in a saucer and let it warm a little before serving it to your kitten. Equally, never serve fresh food scalding hot from the oven or pan; always allow it to cool down before it is offered as your kitten's meal.

Problems with Faddy Eaters

Most kittens will eat what they are given unless they are feeling poorly or off-colour. As with humans, some cats prefer one food to another, and this should be no cause for worry unless it makes for an unbalanced diet. Cats do like variety in their diet, so try to get your kitten used to all sorts of different fresh foods, as well as the assorted brands and flavours of tinned food. This way, if your kitten goes off one particular food, you can always give it another.

Do not pander to your kitten too much, however. If it is fit and healthy, it will be hungry and will eventually eat what is put in front of it. If you spoil it at mealtimes, you are going to have both feeding and dietary problems for a long time to come! You would not consider it very healthy for a young child to eat only fish fingers and baked beans, so think of your kitten's diet in the same way and start as you mean to go on, by being firm!

In the summer heat, cats and kittens quite often go off their food, and this is no cause for alarm: don't you often feel the same when it is very hot, and only fancy a little bit of salad or something like

Raw fresh meat for a kitten – it has just been slightly browned under the grill

it? If your kitten refuses to eat, take the food bowl away, especially in hot weather when flies are likely to be attracted by the offer of a free meal. Try putting the food bowl back in the cool of the evening and, most likely, you will find your kitten tucking in quite happily.

In the unlikely event that your kitten refuses to eat for more than forty-eight hours, it is wise to seek your vet's advice, as there may be a physical reason that is causing the loss of appetite.

Where to Feed Your Kitten, and Suitable Food Containers

Where you decide to feed your kitten is up to you. It should be done in a place that you find convenient, but never at your own dinner table. Bear in mind that cats can be messy eaters, especially where fresh meat is concerned: their natural instincts make them think this is 'prey' that they have caught, and they will want to drag it away in order to eat it out of sight! Fortunately, this does not often happen when canned foods are offered. Cats are not stupid, and realise the difference between a convenience food and one that they could, conceivably, have caught on the hoof!

Once you have decided where your kitten is to eat, it may become difficult to persuade it to eat elsewhere, so do make sure from the outset that you and your family are happy with the feline feeding arrangements. The kitchen is an obvious choice, as it is usually an uncarpeted area that is easy to clean. In a large kitchen, a special corner of the floor area can be given over as your kitten's 'dining room'; in a small kitchen, this is not so practicable, as you will be forever tripping over food and water bowls if they are on the floor, so put them on a work surface out of the way.

Your kitten's water bowl should be kept in the same place: water is vital to all living creatures, and your kitten should know where it will be able to find water at all times.

Do resist the temptation to feed your kitten titbits from your dining table. It may be amusing to your family and friends to see a little kitten looking up longingly as it begs for a bit of your supper, but such a feeding habit will be hard to stop. It is not so funny to have a fully grown cat jump up onto the dining table whenever food is served. If allowed to behave in this way as a kitten, a grown cat will rightly think that this is normal and what you expect it to do. Dinner guests, however, may think differently.

It is sensible to buy special feeding bowls for your kitten, and these should be washed separately from those plates that you and your family use. Try to find feeding bowls that cannot tip over: an excited and hungry kitten may actually try to get into the

food bowl, spilling the contents and covering itself with food that, most likely, it will then tread all over your home. Do not buy bowls that are too large, as they will cause the same problems when your kitten tries to lick out the last bits of its meal from an inaccessible corner!

Plastic bowls are most commonly found in pet stores, but they do not last very long, can be chewed through easily, and will not stand up to frequent washing for more than a year or so. Metal feeding bowls, although more expensive, are a good investment as they are almost indestructible, will take unlimited washing (even in a dish-washer), and can be sterilised in boiling water if need be.

Look also for bowls that will stack on top of each other easily, as this will lessen considerably the amount of storage space you have to give over to feline paraphernalia in your cupboards – and who ever has enough cupboard space?

Finally, when feeding your kitten, it is a good idea to put the food and water bowls on a tray. This will minimise any spillage to a small area. Kittens do tend to push their food bowls along as they eat, and if these are placed on a tray, it will stop the kitten moving the food around too much. It will also make it easier for you to pick up the dirty bowls for washing, and to keep the floor clean.

Stealing from the table

SHOWING YOUR KITTEN

Cat shows, as we know them today, have been in existence for a little over a hundred years. There are records of cats being exhibited at a fair in Winchester, England as far back as 1598, but the first cat show for specially bred pedigree exhibits was organised by Harrison Weir on 13 July 1871. This show, held at the Crystal Palace in London, attracted 160 exhibits which were judged to a specified standard, known as the 'points of exhibition'. These were very similar to the 'standard of points' that judges are still using today, although the types now required in the various breeds have altered considerably!

In 1887, Harrison Weir felt that a general administrative body should be set up to keep records of pedigrees and generally oversee the running of cat shows, and so, in that year, the National Cat Club was founded.

A hundred years on, in 1987, the National Cat Club celebrated its centenary at its annual show held at Olympia in London. The format of the show may have changed very little, but the number of exhibits certainly has: in 1987, there were 2,227 entries in the pedigree section, as well as 318 cats and kittens entered in the pet section alone!

Today, cat shows are a common occurrence in most countries throughout the world, but the way they are organised and administered does vary from country to country.

Cat Shows in the United Kingdom
Shows in the UK are run under the rules of the Governing Council of the Cat Fancy and during the course of a year about one hundred of these events are organised by various cat clubs. Some of the shows are for single breeds only, whilst the majority are for all breeds, and most shows also have a section for pet cats of unknown parentage.

The GCCF licenses cat shows under three general headings. Exemption shows are usually small affairs and can quite often be found as part of a general agricultural show. Although they are run along the guidelines laid down by the GCCF, they do not have to abide by their rules.

Sanction and championship shows have to conform to all the rules and regulations laid down by the GCCF, and both are run in exactly the same

The National Cat Club annual show in London

way, except for the fact that at a sanction show no challenge certificates are awarded. If a club successfully runs three sanction shows, it is usually granted a licence to stage a full championship show and, for this reason, sanction shows are popularly considered to be dress rehearsals for the larger event to follow.

The one exception to this rule is the annual sanction show run by the Kensington Kitten and Neuter Cat Club, where, as there are no entire adult cats present, no challenge certificates can be given, but the winning neuter exhibits may be awarded premier certificates.

How to Find out When and Where
Cat Shows are Held
The show year runs from June to May, and at the beginning of January each year the GCCF publishes a list of all the forthcoming shows that it has licensed. This list can be purchased from the GCCF head office. The official weekly magazine for the GCCF is *Cats*, and the list is also published in the first issue of each new year.

The chronological show list gives all the information you need in the following order: type of show (i.e. championship); if there is to be a non-pedigree section; name of the club running the show; name and address of the show manager; the venue at which the show is to be held.

How to Enter a Show
Look through the show list and find a show that would be suitable for your kitten. If your kitten is a pedigree, there will doubtless be a special annual show for your particular breed, and this would be a good starting point. Otherwise, try to select a show with a venue that is not too far away from your home: your first show will probably be quite an experience for both you and your kitten, so try to keep travel to a minimum or you will end the day feeling completely exhausted!

Having selected the show of your choice, write to the show manager requesting a schedule. These are usually available about three months before the show date, and you should always enclose a large, first-class-stamped, self-addressed envelope so that the schedule and entry form can be posted to you. It is not necessary to be a member of the club in order to enter the show, but there are benefits if you decide to join. Some cat clubs will automatically send members their schedules, and this is quite often a week before they are generally available. Others will afford the same consideration to exhibitors who attended the previous year's show.

The size of the venue governs the number of cats that can be accepted for competition, and acceptance of entries is done strictly on a 'first come, first served' basis: the earlier you receive your schedule, the sooner it can be filled in and returned to the manager – again first-class post is recommended!

The schedule will give all the rules of the show and a list of the classes available. Read this carefully before beginning to complete the entry form. If you have a registered, pedigree kitten (and all the formal requirements of transfer have been completed and accepted), you will be required to give the following details: the kitten's full, registered name; breed number; sex; date of birth; name of sire and dam; and the name of the breeder. All this information will appear on both the pedigree and transfer forms supplied when you bought the kitten, and should be copied very carefully.

In order for you to show the kitten, it must be registered in your name with the GCCF. If you do not have documentation to this effect, contact the breeder immediately so that the kitten can be officially transferred to your ownership.

If your kitten is a non-pedigree, there will probably be little that you know about it, so you only have to fill in its pet name, coat colour, and approximate age or date of birth – a much less daunting task!

Classes at cat shows fall into three categories: open, miscellaneous (or side), and club classes. Your kitten must be entered in its appropriate open as well as, usually, at least three other classes. Pedigree open classes will be listed in sections: these are Longhair, British Shorthair, Foreign Shorthair, Burmese and Siamese. For each breed, and often each colour, there will be open classes for each adult, neuter and kitten of either sex.

In larger shows, the kitten class may also be sub-divided by age, so do make sure that you have the correct date of birth. If you have a problem with the open class, ask your kitten's breeder to help you.

Non-pedigree kittens also have open classes, but these are usually much easier to understand: Longhair or Shorthair, male or female and, at larger shows, different coat colours, and that is about all.

Miscellaneous classes for pedigree kittens allow different breeds to compete together within their own section, so, for example, in the Foreign Shorthair section, these classes will allow a Russian Blue and an Abyssinian to be judged against each other. There are many categories of class within the miscellaneous section, ranging from debutante, for kittens that have never been shown before, to limit, for those that have won no more than four first prizes: the definition of the classes available is always printed in the schedule, and careful reading will ensure that you do not make a mistake.

In the non-pedigree section, miscellaneous classes are 'fun' ones, with such titles as 'the kitten with the biggest eyes' or 'the kitten the judge would

Vetting in

most like to take home'! Finally, if you are a fully paid-up member of a cat club, you may find that your club has offered a special class that your kitten can enter.

Having noted the classes that you wish to enter, write the class numbers in the appropriate boxes on the entry form and sign to confirm that, to the best of your knowledge, all the information is correct. With this completed form, you should enclose your cheque for the entry fees, benching (that is the rental of the pen in which your cat or kitten sits), entry passes and catalogue, and if you wish to receive confirmation that the entry has been accepted, you should also enclose a stamped, addressed postcard, which can then be returned to you.

This task completed, and posted off to the show manager, your thoughts should now be on the show, what equipment is needed and what will be required of you on show day!

What Equipment is Necessary
By now, you should already have a sturdy cat-carrying box and the grooming equipment suitable for your particular kitten. You will also need a white, non-cellular show blanket, white litter tray, disinfectant, cotton wool, shirring elastic (or white ribbon) for the tally which is hung round the kitten's neck, and white food and water containers. These, invari-

ably, can be purchased from one of the trade stands at the show, but, if at all possible, they should be bought in advance.

Your kitten will also require food, water and litter to see it through the day. You may prefer to bring along your kitten's favourite titbit for its lunch, but you will find that many brands of cat food can be purchased at the show – do not forget to bring your can opener!

Water is freely available and, unless your kitten is accustomed only to bottled mineral water, it will not be necessary to carry this with you. At some show venues, however, the water supply is not so easy to find, so some exhibitors still prefer to take their own supply! Cat litter is heavy to carry, so it is easier to buy a small quantity of this when you arrive at the show hall.

Increasingly, cat shows are being sponsored by the manufacturers of cat food, so you may well find that you are given a 'goody bag' containing food and litter to keep your kitten happy through the day!

If the show is held during the cold winter months, you may like to bring a hot water bottle to keep your kitten warm, but this must be placed well out of sight under the white show blanket. All show equipment must look, within reason, the same: any distinguishing or coloured items in the show pen could result in your kitten being disqualified.

Preparing Your Kitten for the Show

If you have followed the advice on grooming, there is little more that you can do. A kitten that has not been regularly groomed and cared for cannot be transformed overnight! Make sure that you have all the items of equipment packed and ready for an early start in the morning. Your kitten will have to go through an inspection by an independent veterinarian, so ensure that the eyes and ears are clean.

It is a GCCF requirement that all entries are inoculated against FIE at least seven days prior to the show, and evidence of this may be requested, so make sure that you take the inoculation certificate with you.

Finally, as judges do not enjoy being scratched, it is a kindly thought to trim your kitten's claws a little, so that, if it were to become nervous, it will not cause any irreparable damage to the judge or steward!

What to Do at the Show

The doors open for exhibitors from 7.30 am onwards and the first thing you must do is collect your tally envelope. This contains a small white tally disc, with your kitten's pen number on it, a vetting-in card, and your prize card listing the classes entered. A few shows will send these out in advance and if this is the case, it will say so in the schedule, requesting you to enclose an SAE with the entry form, for this purpose.

You will now be directed to one of the veterinary surgeons, who will examine your kitten for any sign of parasites, such as fleas and ear mites, and make sure that it is generally in good health. Any sign of illness will result in the exhibit being rejected from the show and the owner will have to get a clearance certificate from his or her own vet, stating that the kitten has fully recovered, before entering another show.

If the vet passes your kitten as fit and healthy, he will sign the vetting-in card. Some shows will have a check-out table, where you must hand in the card, and where an official will mark your kitten as present.

Following the number on the tally, you must now find your kitten's pen. These are arranged in numerical order to make the task easier, but if you have difficulty, there are usually officials present at the show to help you. Having located your pen, it is a good idea to wipe the inside over with some cotton wool moistened with a little disinfectant. The pens have all been steam-cleaned, but it is always better to be on the safe side. (Aerosol sprays are not allowed).

Place the litter tray, litter and kitten in the pen, and leave the kitten there for a while – it may have a necessary function to perform! Thereafter, tie the tally around your kitten's neck with the elastic or ribbon (not too tightly), arrange the blanket so that it is comfortable for your kitten, clean the litter tray

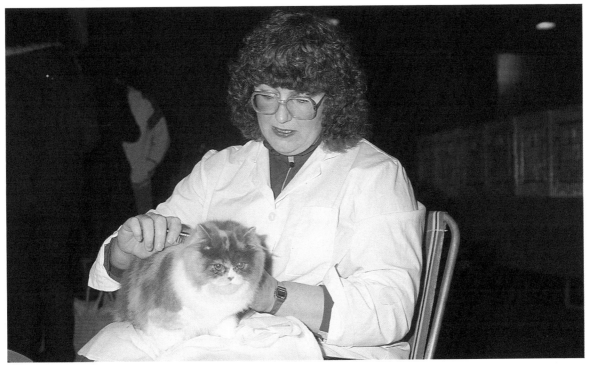

Grooming at a show

as necessary, and put the water bowl in the pen.

If your kitten is hungry and you decide to feed it, do remember to take the food bowl out of the pen before judging commences. You may like to give your kitten a final brush and comb while you have time. If you have a longhaired breed, make sure that any trace of talculm powder has been brushed out of the coat as this could lead to disqualification.

At 10.00 am, you will be asked to leave the hall so that the judges can start work. Ensure that any food, food bowls or toys have been removed from the pen as they could be construed as distinguishing marks by the judge and can result in disqualification. Catalogues will be available for sale at this time and you will thus be able to see what competition your kitten is up against.

Results for the open classes usually start coming up about 11.30 am, and these will be placed on a board for all to see. The result slips show the pen numbers of the exhibits in numerical order, against which the judge will have written the placings. These are, in descending order, 1st, 2nd, 3rd, 4th, VHC (very highly commended), HC (highly commended) and C (commended). CNH against an exhibit's pen number is the abbreviation for 'could not handle', and means that the judge could not remove the cat from its pen for assessment.

At the bottom of the slip there can be a BOB, followed by a pen number. This is the entry that the judge considers best of breed, and this will have been chosen from the 1st-prize-winning male and female of each breed. In the adult section, the 1st-prize winners will have either CC or CC w/h against the placing. This means that the judge has either awarded, or withheld, the challenge certificate.

In a similar way, the neuter adult winners will have either PR or PR w/h, indicating the awarding or withholding of the premier certificate. Cats, and neuters, that have won three of these certificates from different judges, can use the title champion or premier in front of their names. Although these cats may compete along with others of the same breed in the open, there is a special champion of champions class (and premier of premiers) where they compete against other champions within their section for the grand challenge certificate. Three of these awards from different judges allow the title of grand champion/premier to be used – the ultimate accolade in the cat world!

During the course of the afternoon, the results of the other classes will come up, rosettes and prize cards will be placed on the pens and, if there is to be a best in show, tension will be mounting! The BOB winners in each section are judged against each other and, at the end of the day, there will be a BIS

adult, neuter and kitten for each of the five pedigree sections, as well as a BIS neuter and kitten for the non-pedigrees. Not all shows have a BIS, and some arrange it in a slightly different way, but this method of selection is the most common.

Some shows will give out prize money and/or rosettes for the side classes, and this is where your prize card comes in useful: sometimes you may be unable to collect your prizes without it! There may also be cups, trophies and specially donated prizes to be awarded as well.

What the Judges Look for

The judge will assess each entry both in and out of its pen. In the UK, the judge goes to the cat and not the other way round, as is usual in many other countries, and he or she will have an assistant, known as a steward, to help. The steward's duties are many, not the least of which is to push a wheeled table along. The judge will want to examine the cat carefully, and a mobile table for the exhibit to stand on allows such close examination.

The exception to this is the annual GCCF Supreme Show, where a ring-judging system operates. Here the exhibitors are allowed to decorate their cats' pens, as judging takes place away from the main area, and a steward will remove each cat from its pen when the judge is ready for its particular class. There are no side classes at this show, and the eventual overall winner will be allowed to use the title 'supreme' in front of any other titles it has gained.

In order to enter the Supreme, a cat or kitten must have qualified for the show; adults and neuters must either be full champions or premiers, or have gained at least one CC or PC during the preceding show year, and kittens must have had at least one open class win during the same period.

For each breed, there is a standard of points (SOP), and the judge must assess the cat to the standards laid down. Consideration will also be given to health, condition, temperament and presentation: if two exhibits conform to the standard equally, but one has been groomed better, has a more equable temperament, or even a cleaner blanket, this will be reflected in the judge's final placings. In the non-pedigree section, where there are no breed standards, the exhibits can only be judged for their appeal, friendliness, condition, grooming and presentation.

Cat Shows in Other Countries

Whatever the country, the purpose of a cat show remains the same: the judges are looking for the best example of each breed and if the standard of the exhibit is worthy, they will help it on its way

A successful non-pedigree

The judge (left) goes to the cat, not vice versa, in UK
shows

An Australian cat show

to becoming a champion. The main difference between the UK and the rest of the world lies in the way in which shows are run, the terminology used, and the method employed in order for a cat to become a champion.

The preparation for the show, the equipment required, schedules, entry form and catalogues are still pretty much the same, although coloured drapes and blankets are used to decorate the pens in most countries other than the UK. In the UK this is quite forbidden.

European Shows

The largest governing body in Europe is FIFe (*Fédération Internationale Féline*), and most European shows are run under its rules. As in the UK, certificates may be awarded to the best cat of each breed, with three such, awarded by different judges, entitling the cat to be known as a champion.

Equally, there is a special class for these champions to compete with each other for a grand championship. A CAC (*Certificat d'Aptitude de Championnat*) is the equivalent to the British CC, with the higher CACIB (*Certificat d'Aptitude de Championnat International de Beauté*) corresponding to a grand challenge certificate. The cats are exhibited in decorated pens, with judging taking place either in a separate room or in another part of the hall.

There is considerable liaison between the GCCF and FIFe, and European judges are often invited to judge at British shows and vice versa. This is a most welcome development.

Australian Shows

These are run on the same lines as UK shows except for small differences, e.g. the minimum age for kittens is only ten weeks (twelve in UK), and side classes are different too. Ring judging was being evaluated during 1987 and 1988. Australian fanciers often have to work in difficult circumstances owing to climate, distance etc. and are to be congratulated on the successes they have achieved.

South African Shows

Shows in South Africa are held on almost the same lines as those in the UK. In most cases the judges take their 'stands' to the cages. However, some of the seven clubs have tried a modified ring system and have the judges seated at tables in a separate room, the cats being brought to them in containers by the stewards.

Standards and rules are based on those of the GCCF. Judges report on every cat judged by them and a complete set of reports is sent to every exhibitor and all other judges. All clubs include a section for domestic pets in their shows.

American Shows

There are several governing bodies in the USA, but the main one is the CFA, or Cat Fanciers' Association. As in Europe, the ring judging system is employed and the exhibits are allowed to have highly decorated pens, because judging is carried out in another part of the hall. Under CFA rules, a worthy cat can become a champion at a single show. If one judge feels that the cat has sufficient merit for the award, it is only necessary for two other judges to confirm this opinion, and the title is granted.

The Judge's Report

The main reason for taking your kitten to a show is to get the judge's appraisal of its quality. In the UK, where the open class judging is done when the exhibitors are not present, the reports will appear in *Cats* magazine approximately four to six weeks after the show date. The Supreme is the one exception, where the judges' written comments will be placed on the cats' pens. Most judges will be happy to give you their comments on your kitten at the show, but you must never approach or speak to a judge while judging is still in progress.

At European shows, the judge will provide a written report on each exhibit, which is displayed on the pen for all to see.

'Public' judging is the norm at US shows, and here the judge will give a verbal appraisal of each exhibit in front of an audience, as well as writing out a score sheet of the points awarded.

BREEDING FROM YOUR CAT

The idea of breeding from your cat, and bringing new little kittens into the world, is an exciting proposition, but one that requires serious consideration on your part. If you decide to breed from your cat, you have a very real moral responsibility to ensure that the resulting kittens are properly fed and cared for, as well as being certain that you can find suitable homes for them when they are old enough to leave their mother. A large number of unwanted cats and kittens are abandoned each year, and you must not allow yourself to add to this problem by breeding kittens on a whim.

Do you Really Want to Breed from Your Cat?

Breeding cats is, on the whole, a time-consuming, expensive and unprofitable venture and there is little justification for the breeding of non-pedigree felines. Accidents do happen, however, and a look around any cat sanctuary or rescue home will reveal all manner of 'moggy' cats and kittens that have been abandoned and need a new home, so it is hardly sensible deliberately to breed more kittens like this.

Also, think of the situation you are putting your poor little female in. Left calling, outside, she will attract all the local toms, and the male of the feline species is not renowned for his gentle courtship.

It is true that pedigree cats can be abandoned too, but generally this is rarer. If someone is prepared to pay something like a week's wages or more for a kitten, the chances are that they are going to look after it well, as the price, for most of us, is quite considerable! Wouldn't you tend to take more care of a brand new shiny Mercedes that cost you an arm and a leg, rather than an old banger that was given to you for nothing?

Sadly, this is often the way people view a common or garden moggy. It still makes just as reliable and faithful a friend as a more costly pedigree cat would, but when the owner gets fed up with it, or something goes wrong, it is easily dumped without great financial loss.

A true ailurophile would not dream of such behaviour, but unfortunately there are many other people who do not consider a mere cat to be of much importance, and would abandon one for no greater reason than avoiding the expense of a boarding cattery while they go on holiday, or if, heaven forbid, it was found to be pregnant.

Burmese queen with her new litter

There is much to be gained from the companionship of any cat, pedigree or otherwise, but ownership must be on the basis of undertaking a lifetime's responsibility; so think on – do you really need to breed from your cat? Could you cope with taking one of your kittens back into your home if the new owners changed their minds? As you will be responsible for breeding the kittens, you must also be prepared to find new homes for them if something should go amiss.

Now contemplate the cost of all this. There will be a stud fee to pay, which will vary depending on the breed and status of the male cat concerned: a champion or grand champion will command a higher fee than a stud that has not had a lot of show success. You will also, in many circumstances, have to get an FeLV test done on your queen before the mating is allowed to take place.

There will be the cost of a special high-protein diet, and the necessary vitamin and mineral supplements that the pregnant queen requires. From about four weeks onwards, the kittens will need special food as they will no longer be able to get the necessary nourishment from their mother's milk.

There is also the cost of the extra heating needed if the kittens are born in the winter, more cat litter (kittens do tend to use more than an adult cat!), and the cost of registration fees with the local cat council.

Inoculations will have to be administered at about ten to twelve weeks old, advertisements will have to be placed to find good homes, and what if something goes wrong and you have to call out the vet? Veterinary treatment can be very expensive. A rough breakdown of the finances for rearing a litter to, say, twelve weeks old, reveals that the expenditure comes under at least the following main headings:

Stud fee

FeLV testing

Registrations

Inoculations

Extra heating for 12 weeks

Extra cat litter for 12 weeks

Feeding

Advertising kittens for sale

Stationery (pedigrees, diet sheets etc.)

Vitamin and mineral supplements

If a commercial view is taken, as it should be if you hope to make breeding a profitable affair, you have also to add to your expenses the 'depreciation' of your mother cat and the cost of keeping her and feeding her with a special diet while she produces, if you work her rather too hard, two litters a year. These costs will entirely wipe out any hope of profitability.

The way to make a profit is, alas, to ensure that the queens are worn out by producing kittens as often as possible under 'battery hen' conditions, on the minimum survival diet, and discarded as soon as they become 'useless'.

Some breeders can break even by becoming experts, and keeping popular stud cats and several breeding queens, so that they become renowned for the quality of their stock, which command high prices. The rest regard breeding as a delightful time-consuming hobby and bear the losses with the same equanimity as amateurs bear the time and expense involved in playing tennis or golf.

These are the minimum expenses that will be incurred and it does not take a great home economist to realise that the total profit – assuming no accidents – would be pretty small.

It is unlikely, with your first litter, that you will manage without consulting a vet at some point. Your queen may even develop one of several illnesses that can arise during pregnancy and lactation. It is also just as possible that not all your kittens will survive long enough to be sold. And all of this is without taking into consideration the cost of your time and effort.

Any economist would call this a most unprofitable venture, as it does not give a good return for expenditure incurred. So why do it? There can only be one possible answer – love, coupled with an interest in breeding to improve your own stock and, eventually, the breed as a whole. If you think that there is any other reason for breeding kittens, forget it now.

Neutering, and the Best Age for the Operation

If you decide that the idea of breeding from your cat is not a good one, then you must have your kitten neutered.

For a male, this is a very simple operation, involving a short amount of time under a general anaesthetic, during which the testicles will be removed from the scrotal sac. If you wish your male kitten to grow into a 'butch-looking' adult, defer the operation until the kitten is fully mature. Otherwise, a tom kitten may be neutered from five months onwards. Your kitten will show little by way of immediate side effects, and will most likely be up and bouncing around within twelve hours.

A latent side effect to this operation is a bonus to you as the owner. Entire tom cats tend to wander, spraying their rather offensive-smelling urine to mark their territory wherever they go, and your home will be no exception to this rule! Neutered cats spray more rarely, and so will help you to keep your home smelling sweet!

With a female kitten, the operation, known as spaying, takes slightly longer, as it involves the removal of both the uterus and ovaries and, again, a general anaesthetic will be necessary. It is important to inform the veterinary surgery if the kitten is calling for a mate, as this is an inappropriate time for the operation to be carried out. The kitten will be a little woozy for twenty-four hours or so after the operation, as she will have been under the anaesthetic for a longer time than is needed for a male castration. She should be kept warm, quiet and away from other animals during this period, but you will find that she is back to normal after a couple of days. About a week after the operation she will have to be returned to the vet for the stitches to be removed unless, of course, dissolving stitches have been used.

Although the operation can be performed from four months of age onwards, it is best left until the kitten is at least six months old. By this time she will be sexually mature and the removal of the reproductive organs will not cause any problems later in life. Spaying too early can result in hormonal problems, such as miliary eczema, and for either sex, premature neutering can cause stunting of growth.

If, however, you have both a male and female kitten of similar ages (or even a brother and sister from the same litter) – be careful! Cats do not have moral standards as we know them, and it is quite likely that the two will mate together without either your prior knowledge or, indeed, consent! If the kittens are sexually precocious, but really too young to be neutered, ask your vet to prescribe a feline 'contraceptive pill' (yes, such a thing exists!), until the female can be spayed, or until the male is of an age to be castrated.

Choosing the Right Stud

If all of this has not put you off the idea of breeding from your cat, then you must start to think about finding a suitable stud for your queen. With a maiden queen, it is a good idea to try to find a stud that is not too far away from your home; cats are prone to stress, and mating for the first time will be a stressful experience which will not be helped by a long journey as well. It is not unknown for a cat go 'off call' while travelling a great distance and this will result in the stud cat being completely uninterested in her when she finally arrives at his home.

The distance, however, is only one of the criteria to be contemplated. The pedigrees of both your kitten and any prospective suitors must be studied carefully, taking care not to select a stud that is too closely related to your own kitten. (Experienced breeders will do this occasionally to improve the type, but it is not something to be recommended to a novice.)

The best way to find a suitable stud is to ask the advice of your kitten's breeder, who, if experienced, should be able to assist you in selecting the right mate for your kitten, and should be able to explain the genetic implications of any mating, and what colour variations can be expected in the resulting litter. Most breeders are very helpful and friendly, but in the event that you have not bought your kitten from such a person, the next best thing is either to contact the owner of what seems a suitable stud, or the breed club for your particular breed of kitten, and seek their advice.

Before you take a final decision, make an appointment to visit the stud's premises: your queen will be staying with him for at least two or three days, and, if a maiden, she could be with him for up to a week. Satisfy yourself that your queen will be happy, that the stud seems gentle, that the stud house has safe 'queen's quarters', and that the general standard of hygiene is sound. If you are happy with the arrangements, then look no further, but if you have any qualms whatsoever, go back to stage one and start looking again!

Once you have decided on the stud, and the owner has agreed to the mating, you must expect a barrage of questions from the stud owner! These are only to safeguard the interests of both yourself and the stud owner, as well as the health and well being of your queen and the stud. The sort of questions you should expect to be asked are as follows:

Is the queen registered in your name? (If she is not, you must apply for transfer of ownership as soon as possible.)

What is the queen's pet name? (Few owners call their cat by its proper name, and the use of the pet name will make the cat feel more at home.)

Has the queen been FeLV tested, and what was the date of the last test? (Not all stud owners require this, but the majority do – you may also be asked if other feline members of your household have had this test.)

When did your queen last receive an FIE/cat 'flu vaccination, and what type of vaccine was used? (Your queen should be covered for immunity to these infections from the time that she goes to stud, until the time that the kittens are ready to leave home at twelve weeks old: it is dangerous for her and her kittens to receive any booster inoculation whilst she is either pregnant or lactating. If, from the inoculation certificate, you see that your queen's immunity

A recently spayed queen – the operation leaves a temporary patch of short fur on her flank

is going to run out during this period, have the booster shot administered at least three weeks before you take her to the stud: a recently inoculated cat will shed the virus under stress, but a three-week time lapse will ensure that the inoculation is safe.)

Has your queen been on the 'pill', and has she had a complete call since being taken off the pill? (Feline contraceptive pills work in a similar way to human ones, and it is always advisable to let the queen have a full call before being mated.)

Lastly, you will be asked about the general health, fitness and weight of the queen, and if she has any special dietary requirements or preferences.

When to Have Your Queen Mated

Your kitten may start to call as early as sixteen weeks old, but this is obviously far too young for her to be mated. About nine months old is usually the earliest you should think about mating your queen, but this does also depend on her size, weight and condition. It is a good idea to take your kitten for a veterinary inspection to ensure that she is ready to go to stud. If you get the OK, then all you have to do now is wait for her to come into call . . . and this should not be hard to detect!

An entire female cat is not called a queen for royalist reasons. The name is derived from the Old English word 'quean', meaning a whore or hussy, and your little cat will leave you in no doubt that she is ready to be mated! She will start making strange noises, not unlike a baby crying (hence the term 'calling'); she will roll over and over on the floor; she will assume a strange posture, with her shoulders down, her tail towards one side, and, if you tickle the base of her spine just above the tail, she will start to 'paddle' with her back legs. This is the time to ring the stud owner and confirm that your cat is ready to be mated. You will then be told when to bring her in.

The stud owner will let you know when your queen has been successfully mated, and when she will be ready for collection. You will be given a mating certificate, which will state the date of mating, the date the kittens are expected, and the stud cat's full pedigree. The stud owner will be just as concerned as yourself as to the outcome of the mating (after all, it is a dual venture!), so do keep in contact to let him or her know how the situation is progressing.

Care and Diet During Pregnancy

About twenty-one days after the mating, you should be able to tell if your queen has 'taken', and is now

Mating: the tom grips the queen by the scruff of the neck

Pregnant queen with nipples clearly visible

pregnant. The easiest way to detect this is to examine her nipples. These are normally pale in colour, but if they now appear quite obviously pink, you have a pregnant cat on your hands that now requires a special diet with vitamin and mineral supplements!

If you are in any doubt, take the cat along to your vet, as he or she will be able to feel any kittens at this time (later, the developing foetuses will be protected by fluid, and it will become more difficult to confirm any pregnancy). It is advisable to add extra calcium to the normal diet, as this will help to promote strong bones in the developing kittens. Suitable powders are available from your veterinarian or a good pet store, and these will provide the ideal calcium supplement.

The gestation period for cats is sixty-five days and, surprisingly, cats usually deliver on schedule. A few days before the impending birth, you should prepare a kittening box. There are various ways of making this, but the simplest is to find a good, sturdy cardboard box, place a heated pad or something similar at the bottom, and then line the box with several alternating layers of newspaper and linen. The newspaper will absorb the fluids expelled during the birth, while the linen will keep the queen and kittens comfortable. By using layers of the two, you will be able to remove a soiled section after each kitten is born, without upsetting the mother cat unduly.

Cats do have a trying habit of selecting their own little corner for the birth of their kittens, and unless you really want this happy event to take place in a wardrobe or drawer, you must try to cajole her into your way of thinking and to select a place that is convenient for you. This may not be easy, but do try!

The Birth

Most cats will produce kittens with the greatest of ease, and will purr away happily throughout the course of the birth. Any animal that is designed to produce a multiple birth is going to have a much easier time than one, like a human, who tends to produce just one huge offspring. The space taken up in the uterus will be the same proportionally, but how much easier it is to push out four or five little ones, than one great big one!

For this reason, it is almost unheard of for a cat to need a cut and stitches – the kittens tend to pop out like shelled peas! This does not mean that you should not be present, indeed this is all important, as a novice queen may not know quite what to do. Be prepared, in case you need to help, and items that can come in handy are:

    clean towels
    sterilised scissors
    boiled water
    a hot water bottle (just in case there is a weak or sickly kitten that needs extra heat)

. . . and a friend to help you and keep your blood pressure down!

Lastly, do let your vet know when your queen is due to kitten, and if he or she is to be off duty that day, make sure that you have the telephone number of his or her locum. Many cats revert to their wild instincts for the birth, and will only produce their kittens under cover of darkness when few predators would be around. It is a kind thought to warn your vet of the impending birth, so that he or she will be prepared for a midnight 'phone call if anything goes wrong!

A day or so before the birth, your cat will start to 'nest', and this is when you should try to persuade her that your choice of kittening box is the best, and safest, place for her to give birth. This should be heated with a special pet bed heater, or with a series of hot water bottles (the latter are not very convenient, as you will have to keep changing them, and there is always the possibility that one might burst). Heated pads are not expensive, and are a good investment for any future litters.

Make sure that the box is situated in a quiet, dark corner of your home and that if you have children, they are told to keep away. Contractions may start well before the birth, and these should be watched carefully. When the waters break, this indicates that the first kitten is due very shortly. You will notice a 'bubble' appearing at the opening of the vagina: this is the first kitten, and your queen is now in the final stages of labour. The contractions will get stronger and more frequent until the kitten is finally born. Do not worry if the kitten comes out tail first; this is perfectly normal and you may find several kittens are presented in this manner.

The mother will immediately begin to lick the kitten hard. This removes the amniotic sac, dries the kitten's fur, and stimulates its circulation. The placenta (or afterbirth) should be expelled from the uterus at this time. The kitten will still be attached to it by means of the umbilical cord, and the mother will chew through this to separate the two. If she wants to eat the placenta, and not all cats do, let her go ahead but do not let her eat too many as this can cause diarrhoea. The kitten will now try to find its way to the nearest nipple, and should start to suckle.

The mother cat may have a little rest before the next delivery, or just continue until all the kittens have been born. It is important to make sure that all the placentas have been expelled from the uterus, so make sure you account for one placenta for each kitten. If a placenta is left behind, it will begin to decompose, with the result that uterine infection could set in. Should you not be able to account for all the placentas within twenty-four hours of kitten-ing, it would be wise to consult your vet.

When you are sure that all the kittens have been born, gently remove the soiled sheeting, and replace it with clean, dry bedding. Always use smooth sheeting, as it is easy for kittens to get their spiky little claws hooked up in blankets or towelling. Your queen will want to stay close to her kittens, so put a litter tray and water bowl nearby; she may prefer to use a tray away from the immediate vicinity of the kittens, so do make both alternatives available to her and do not worry if she does not want to use the tray at all for the first twenty-four hours after kittening.

If she seems hungry, which she probably will not be if she has eaten any afterbirths, offer her a small, light meal, such as white fish or chicken, and at all times make sure that fresh water is available to her.

The time that this whole procedure takes will vary from cat to cat: there are no hard and fast rules! Depending on the size of the litter, about two to three hours is the norm, but some cats will produce a whole litter in a matter of minutes, while others could take up to twenty-four hours. Unless your cat seems distressed, there is no cause to worry. Violent, painful and non-productive contractions should not be allowed to proceed beyond an hour, and the vet should be called.

What Can Go Wrong During the Birth

Most cats will produce their kittens as described above, but there are some problems that can arise and it is best to be forewarned as you will have to act quickly in most cases.

A maiden queen may be 'confused' when she first goes into labour, and can react in different ways. She may think that she is simply passing a motion, and so try to give birth in the litter tray. Gently move her back to her kittening box, reassure her and, as soon as the kitten is born and the umbilical cord has been severed, persuade her to wash the kitten and get it suckling as quickly as possible –she will soon realise what is going on!

Occasionally, a maiden queen will confuse the kitten with the afterbirth and try to eat the wrong one. Again, once she comes to terms with the reality of the situation, she will soon realise what she is meant to be doing!

If your queen has been in labour for two hours or more without producing a kitten, then it may be that one has become stuck in the birth canal. It is important to contact the vet immediately. It may be possible for him or her to manipulate the kitten's position, so that it can be presented normally, but sometimes a caesarean section may be necessary. An experienced breeder would try to do this manipu-lation, but it is inadvisable for a novice to do so,

The mother immediately starts to lick the kitten vigorously

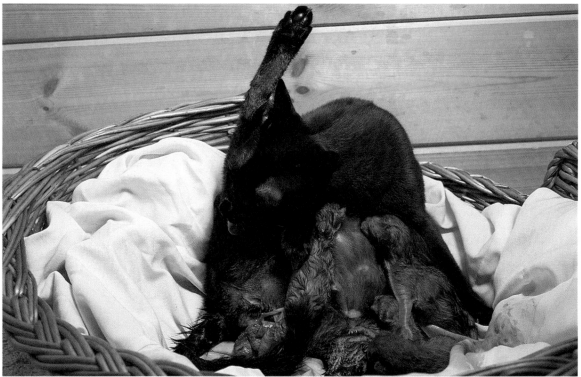

Make sure you can account for a placenta to each each kitten

Day-old kitten suckling

as you would probably do more harm than good.

Sometimes, a queen will start to go into labour and then stop. She may even produce one or two kittens and then appear to give up. This is usually caused by a condition known as uterine inertia, whereby the muscles causing the contractions of the uterus tire and fade. This can easily be confused with a cat who is simply resting between kittens, and purring away contentedly, but one with uterine inertia will seem depressed and uninterested in the whole proceedings, and if she has already produced a kitten, she will most likely ignore it. You will need to call the vet, as he or she can administer an injection of pituitrin and calcium, which will stimulate the muscular contractions and allow birth to proceed as normal.

During the delivery, a kitten can sometimes get stuck half in and half out of the vulva. This is a situation where you may be able to help. Wash your hands thoroughly and apply lubrication to the entrance of the vulva (petroleum jelly is best, but cooking oil or washing-up liquid will do in an emergency!) Try to grasp hold of as much of the kitten as possible, using a towel to aid a firm grip, and gently, but firmly, using a continuous and steady action, pull the kitten free in time with the queen's contractions. You should find that this little bit of extra help will free the kitten, but in the event that

it does not work, you will have to summon veterinary assistance. It is possible that a lot of blood will be emitted during the delivery, but this is perfectly normal and natural, and so should be no cause for worry.

Most mother cats will chew through the umbilical cord with no difficulty at all, but if yours does not, this is where the scissors come in handy. Sterilise them in boiling water, and sever the cord about 2.5 cm (1 in) from the kitten. Never let the queen drag a kitten around while the cord is still attached, as this could cause the kitten to become herniated.

If a kitten appears to be dead on delivery, you will have to act very quickly if it is to be saved. It is most likely that amniotic fluid has got into its lungs, and this must be expelled as quickly as possible. Clean any mucus and traces of the amniotic sac away from the mouth and face. Sever the umbilical cord at least 2.5 cm (1 in) away from the kitten, with the sterilised scissors, and, wrapping the kitten in a towel or something similar, grasp it firmly. Keeping the head pointing downwards and away from you, take the following course of action. Try to think of the way that you would make an overarm bowl in cricket, and do the same, holding the kitten securely in your hand – but don't let go!

Do this two or three times, and then rub the kitten hard with the towel. With a bit of luck, you should hear the kitten choke and splutter as it comes back to life. Continue with this procedure until you are sure that all the fluid has been expelled, and the kitten is breathing normally. (It is quite a good idea to do this out of the sight of the mother, as she may be a bit upset to see such 'rough' handling of one of her babies!)

Finally, there are one or two things that may occur, all of which are perfectly normal and should be no cause for alarm!

1 There is a 'plug' of mucus that usually comes loose shortly before birth: this can come away as early as a week before the kittens are born. Unless there is any greenish discharge, or blood, do not worry!

2 The birth itself is a stressful experience for a kitten, and the pressure exerted during this time can cause the kitten to excrete faeces. If a kitten is born with a dark brown or black secretion from its rear passage, panic not! Many human babies do exactly the same thing.

3 As with any birth, there will be a certain amount of blood involved. This is usually well diluted with amniotic fluid, so it does not look so much bright red, as vaguely pink. It may take the mother some days before these secretions stop, so do not worry if you see slightly blood-stained linen in the kittening box for up to a week after the birth.

After-care and Weaning of the Kittens

For the first few weeks, the mother cat will attend to all maternal duties and there is little for a mere human to do! Make sure that she and her little family are kept warm, dry and comfortable, and that she has her food, water and litter tray adjacent to the kittening box.

Over the next twelve weeks the kittens will change from being blind, helpless little mites, to independent and self-assured small cats, ready to leave their mother and make their way in the big wide world, and settle in with a new owner.

Kittens are born with their eyes closed, and, at about ten days old, these will start to open. For the first three weeks or so, the kittens will rely completely on their mother's milk for food. This will take a lot out of the mother cat so ensure that she receives a good, high-protein diet. It is advisable to administer vitamin and mineral supplements at this time, as well.

About a week after their eyes open, the kittens will start to crawl around inside the nest or kittening box, and at about three weeks old, they should start to climb out. Between three and four weeks, they will start to show an interest in solid food and weaning can begin. The kittens may not all start to eat at the same time, but this is no cause for alarm; it is much easier to have a quick suck from mother

Eyes opening at ten days

than to go through all the bother of chewing food!

Start the kittens on a light diet; finely minced chicken, flaked white fish and tinned or bottled baby foods are all suitable for young kittens. Never offer kittens cow's milk, as it is likely to cause diarrhoea. Instead use either diluted evaporated milk or one of the powdered cat-milk substitutes. (The latter can be bought from a good pet store and should be made up according to the directions given on the tin.)

Once they begin to eat solid foods, the kittens will also begin to use the litter tray. Most kittens will follow their mother's example and use the tray without needing to be toilet trained. If any kittens seem unsure of what the tray is for, put them on it immediately after each mealtime – they will soon get used to the idea! At six weeks, the kittens can be given meat meals, such as finely minced, cooked beef and tinned cat or kitten food. By eight weeks old, they should be fully weaned and no longer suckling from their mother.

At about ten to twelve weeks old, the kittens will need to have their first inoculations. (The time that these are given depends on the size, weight and general condition of the kittens, and on the type of vaccine used.) If the kittens are only being immunised against FIE, there is only one inocula-tion, but combined FIE and cat 'flu protection re-quires two inoculations to be given two to three weeks apart.

Until the kittens are fully immunised, they should not be allowed to go outside or to meet other cats apart from those that live in your household. If the latter are afforded free range or have been exhibited recently at a cat show, where they could have picked up an infection, do not allow contact. An inoculated cat may show no sign of illness, but can carry a live virus that can then be passed on to uninoculated kittens.

Some kittens may show an adverse reaction to the vaccine; this is not usually very serious and will only cause them to be a little off-colour for a day or two, with a possibility of sneezing and runny eyes and noses. For this reason, do not let the kittens go to their new homes until three or four days after the inoculations.

Problems that May Arise while Rearing Kittens

'Dirty Kittens'
Once one kitten begins to urinate or defecate in an area outside the litter tray, all its siblings (and quite

Given a chance, even a fully weaned kitten will still suckle

72

A kitten at seven weeks

likely any adult cats) will follow suit – again, it is the smell that will lead them to the soiled area. The most common reason for this behaviour is either a dirty litter tray (cats are usually very fastidious animals), or not enough trays being available for the litter and the mother too.

There are various proprietary brands of cat repellent available, but few are truly effective. The most successful way to stop this behaviour is to change the environment. If possible, try to put the food bowls over the soiled spot as cats will rarely defecate near their feeding area. This may not be practicable if the chosen toilet area is under the TV, or behind the sofa, in which case deny access by putting, for example, an inverted cardboard box over the spot.

Intussusception

This is not a common condition, but when it does occur, it seems most usually to affect kittens, or queens who have recently given birth. An intussusception is an intestinal problem, whereby a section of the intestine doubles back on itself in a telescopic fashion, rather like turning a sock inside out. In adults, this can be cured by surgery, during which a section of the intestine will be removed. Depending on the severity of the intussusception, this operation can sometimes be performed on kittens, but, in most cases involving young kittens, the prognosis is not hopeful and the chances of recovery are, literally, fifty:fifty.

Lack of Milk

Occasionally, a queen may not have enough milk to go round, or may dry up completely. In this circumstance, the kittens will have to be foster-fed at regular and frequent periods, depending on their age. Cat foster-feeder bottles are commercially available from good pet stores, along with 'cat' milk powder, and these two will help you to cope with the problem. Sterilise and perforate the teats with seven or eight holes to ensure that the milk will flow readily – kittens have very low suction power. As with any products, use them according to the instructions given on the label.

Kittens that are not receiving enough milk will cry continually, and this should alert you to such a problem. It is important to remember to wipe each kitten's bottom with a little kitchen paper after each meal. If their mother is not interested in their welfare, due to a lack of milk, her natural stimulation in this department will be missing.

Litter Eaters

It can sometimes happen that a kitten does not understand what the cat litter is for, and will try to eat it. This usually only happens for a short while until the kitten realises what it should really be doing in the litter tray! If you have this problem, try putting a little urine-soiled litter in the tray – the smell should be enough to persuade your kitten that this is the area to be used as a toilet.

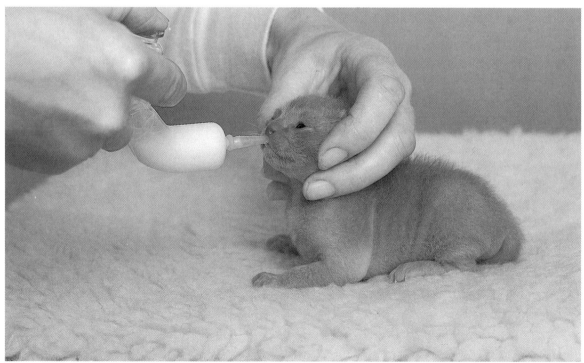

Foster-feeding with a bottle

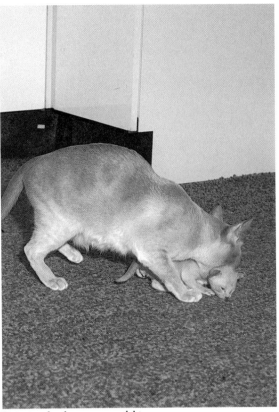

Bringing back a wayward kitten

Mastitis

While a queen is still lactating, it is possible for mastitis to set in. The symptoms, and these may occur within twenty-four hours of infection, are a rise in temperature, a reluctance to feed the kittens, general distress and, most important, a mammary gland that is hard or lumpy, impacted, hot to the touch and unable to produce milk. The milk from the affected gland (usually only one is affected) will be infected, and if that milk is taken in by a kitten, it too will become ill. It is important to prevent any kittens suckling from the mastitic gland and it may be necessary to bandage the affected area if the kittens are unweaned. The queen must be put on a course of antibiotics immediately, so you must contact a vet as soon as possible. Once the gland has healed, and any pus has been evacuated, the kittens may return to this nipple as normal.

Pyometra

This can develop in any entire female cat at any age. The main symptom is a plentiful, cream-coloured secretion from the vulva, accompanied by a rise in temperature and general ill health, increased thirst and loss of appetite. It is also possible for a cat to have a 'closed pyometra', whereby the cervix is tightly closed and so no secretions will be seen. In any event, this is a condition that must be treated by a veterinarian. In mild cases, antibiotics might work, but, in the majority of cases, the queen will have to be spayed.

General Points

Kittens move fast and are rarely lacking in enthusiasm for life. Do make sure that you, the members of your family and visitors are aware of this fact. Walk carefully when kittens are around – it is so easy to tread on them, and bones are easily broken. Never slam a door shut – you could so easily cause a fatal accident. Keep windows closed, or make them escape-proof – you would be surprised at the small space it needs for a kitten to get out.

When disinfecting, and this is necessary to prevent infection, *always* read the instructions on the packet or bottle. Disinfectants are very useful preparations, but they are usually sold in a concentrated form. They must always be diluted according to the manufacturer's recommendations. *Never* use any disinfectant that contains phenols or cresols – these are lethal to cats and must be avoided.

Selling the Kittens

If you do not already have homes for your litter, you will have to think about placing an advertisement to the effect that you have kittens for sale. For the last twelve weeks or so, you will have spent much time having fun and receiving amusement, pleasure and enjoyment from your kittens, and so you will want them to go on to just as loving a home as you have provided for them in these vital first few weeks. It is a heartbreaking time, so do question any would-be owners most thoroughly.

Place the advertisement some weeks before the kittens are ready to go and ask the prospective buyers to come and choose their kitten. It is advisable to take a deposit at this time (say 10 per cent of the total purchase price), to confirm the agreement. This should be partly or wholly refundable in the event of a change of mind from either party – it is better not to sell a kitten at all, than have it returned after a few weeks – but advertisements are not cheap, so make sure that you are covered for the cost of readvertising.

Always ask visitors to wash their hands thoroughly before they touch or handle your kittens. Infections can be passed on so easily that it is sensible to take this simple precaution. If you are happy that the intended owners are suitable for your kitten, then the sale can go ahead! When the time comes for the kitten to be collected, you will then not feel too upset, as you should be sure that it is going to a super new home.

GLOSSARY

agouti the pure golden brown colour that appears in a band on the hairs of Tabby and Abyssinian (and some other) cats. Each hair carries a series of colour bands, creating an overall striped or mottled effect.

ailurophile a cat lover.

ailurophobe a cat hater.

altering the removal of the reproductive organs (USA).

AOC any other colour.

AOV any other variety.

benching the term used to describe the hired pen that your cat or kitten occupies at a cat show.

BIS best in show.

BOB best of breed.

break a term referring to the shape of the nose between the head and the nostrils. In some breeds, such as Burmese, a firm nose break is preferable, but in others, like the Siamese, where a sloping nose line is the required standard, any break in the nose conformation is considered a severe fault.

breed cats of the same genetic origin that, when bred together, will produce the same type.

brood queen a female cat that, although perhaps not a show specimen, is kept for breeding purposes, as her genetic lines are quite sound.

calling a female cat that is ready to mate. Also called being in season or on heat (USA).

castration the surgical removal of the testicles of a male cat.

catnip (*Nepeta cataria*) a herb that cats love, and which they will chew at or roll in. It induces a trance-like state in many cats. It is an easy plant to grow in most gardens.

The Abyssinian has bands of agouti colour on each hair, creating stripes and 'ticking' in the coat colour

Catnip

*The Himalayan factor seen in two Colourpoint kittens
(Blue and Tortoiseshell)*

CC Challenge Certificate, an award issued to the best male and best female of each variety or colour. Three of these, issued by different judges, make the cat a full champion.

CH champion – this may be added in front of the cat's registered name when it has gained three CC's from three different judges.

CFA Cat Fancier's Association (US administrative body).

Championship show a cat show where the best male and the best female of each breed or colour can be awarded a challenge certificate, and premier certificates for the neuters.

CNH could not handle. (This is sometimes found against a cat's pen number on the judge's slip if the cat refused to be handled for assessment.)

coat term used by judges and breeders to describe the fur, e.g. coat colour, coat texture. etc.

cross breeding breeding two, usually pedigree, cats of different breeds or colour together. This can be done either to improve the type of the breed, or to develop a new breed.

cryptorchid a male cat that has undescended testicles. A cryptorchid kitten may be shown, but in an adult cat this is a fault that disqualifies the exhibit from competition.

dam the mother of the kitten.

doctoring another term, less commonly used, for neutering.

dome the term used to describe the top of the head in some breeds, where the standard of points requires the cat to show a rounded shape both in profile and between the ears.

entire an adult male or female cat that has not been neutered.

exemption show a small cat show, often run in conjunction with an agricultural show, which does not have to abide by the GCCF rules.

FCV feline calici virus – one of two infections that are popularly referred to as cat 'flu.

FeLV feline leukaemia virus.

FeLV testing a simple blood test that can detect the presence of FeLV. This test is often required before a queen is accepted to stud, and a veterinary certificate to this effect will have to be produced.

feral a term applied to undomesticated, free-ranging cats. Most usually colonies of these cats are found on industrial sites or in derelict buildings.

flat chested a deformation of the chest whereby the rib cage caves inwards towards the chest cavity and causes difficulty in breathing. It is often accompanied by a deformed spine, which will show a most noticeable dip behind the shoulders.

Flehmen reaction (flehming) a term used to describe the way a cat turns back its lips when it smells something interesting to it, such as another cat's marking of territory.

FIA feline infectious anaemia.

FIE feline infectious enteritis.

FIFe *Fédération Internationale Féline* (the largest European cat council). This was formerly FIFE (*Fédération Internationale Féline d'Europe.*)

FIP feline infectious peritonitis.

FVR feline viral rhinotracheitis (the second form of cat 'flu).

GCCF the Governing Council of the Cat Fancy (the largest UK cat council).

genotype the term used to describe the genetic make up of a cat.

gestation the period of time between conception and birth. For cats, this is sixty-five days.

GR CH grand champion – an entire cat that has become a full champion and, in competition with other champions, has won three grand challenge certificates under three different judges. The highest honour!

GR PR grand premier – as above, but the title awarded to neutered cats.

haw the third eyelid, correctly called the nictitating membrane. As well as having an upper and lower eyelid, a cat has a third one that moves across sideways, starting nearest to the nose. A raised haw may be due to a foreign body in the eye, but can also denote that the kitten is unwell.

heat another term for calling.

Himalayan factor genetic term to describe the restricted coat pattern as seen in Siamese and Colourpoint cats.

hot used to describe a cream cat whose coat colour shows too much orange or red.

household pet a non-pedigree cat for which, at most shows, there is a special section where it can be entered for competition.

hybrid the progeny of cross-breeding.

in-breeding close mating, such as between siblings.

inoculations annual injections given to immunise cats against FIE and cat 'flu. A kitten will be given its first inoculation at about twelve weeks old.

jowls the large cheeks seen in an adult, entire male cat.

junior a cat under two years old.

kink a tail deformation that is considered a fault if visible.

kitten a young cat under nine months of age.

line-breeding mating between mother and son, or father and daughter.

locket a white patch, usually found under the chin, on the chest, in the armpits or between the back legs. This is considered a fault in some breeds.

maiden 1 a cat who has not been mated before; and 2 a cat or kitten who has never been entered in a cat show before.

mating putting a stud and a queen together, with the view to producing kittens.

moggy common, affectionate term for a non-pedigree cat or kitten.

monorchid a male cat with one undescended testicle. As with cryptorchidism, this is acceptable in a kitten, but is a disqualifiable fault in an entire male.

neuter a cat that has had its reproductive organs removed, such as a spayed female or a castrated male.

neutering a surgical operation, performed by a veterinarian, to spay or castrate a cat.

nictitating membrane the haw or third eyelid.

non-self a term used to describe the coat of a cat that is not a solid colour throughout, from hair root to tip.

novice a cat or kitten that has never won a first prize under GCCF rules.

odd-eyed used of white cats, where one eye is orange and the other blue.

oestrus the period during which an entire female

cat is calling and ready to be mated (most commonly used in the USA).

open class a class open to any cats of the same breed or colour, usually split into male and female entries. In the adult section, the winning cats may be awarded challenge or premier certificates if the judge considers them to be worthy.

overshot when the jaw is misaligned, so that the top jaw juts out over the lower jawline.

pads the cushioned soles of the cat's paws.

papers general term encompassing the pedigree, registration and transfer forms, and certificates of inoculations.

PC premier certificate – an award issued to the best neuter of each variety or colour. Three of these, issued by different judges, make the cat a full premier.

pedigree an authenticated form showing four generations of the cat's ancestry, from parents to great, great grandparents, with all the details of the cat's breeding and the registration numbers of the parents and grandparents.

phenotype the outward manifestation of the cat's genetic make up, such as shape of body and head, coat colour and length, etc.

pinking-up expression used when, about twenty-one days after mating, the colour of the queen's nipples changes to a bright pink, indicating that she is pregnant.

points the restriction of coat colour to the face, ears, paws and tail, as is seen in the Siamese breed, amongst others.

polydactyl a cat whose paws carry an extra digit. A pedigree cat with this condition is ineligible for showing.

PR premier – this title may be added in front of the cat's registered name when it has won three premier certificates from three different judges.

prefix a name chosen by a breeder for the exclusive use of own-bred kittens from his or her cattery. The name must be registered with the GCCF, and is written as the first of the given names for all the kittens from that cattery.

quarantine a period of six months during which any cat imported from outside the United Kingdom must remain in a cattery set aside for this purpose. For other countries, the length of quarantine may vary, or, as in most countries, does not apply at all.

queen an entire female cat.

registration the details of a kitten's birth and parentage, which are accepted and authenticated by a governing council.

sanction show a show run under GCCF championship rules, but at which no certificates are issued. The exception to this is the annual Kensington Kitten and Neuter Club Show where, although no

entire adults are present, the winning neuters may be awarded premier certificates.

self a cat with a solid coat colour that is sound from root to tip.

side classes miscellaneous classes where different breeds and colours may compete with each other. No certificates are issued for the winning entries, only prize money or rosettes.

sire the father of the kitten.

SOP standard of points – a list of standards to which a particular breed of pedigree cat must conform, and the basis upon which judging is carried out.

spaying the surgical removal of the reproductive organs of a female cat.

spraying the method by which a cat will mark its territory, by spraying concentrated urine onto, usually, an upright surface such as a wall. This is more usual in entire male cats, but it is not uncommon for both neuters and entire females to spray if they feel their territory is being encroached upon by another cat.

stud an entire male cat kept for the purpose of breeding.

suffix the same as a prefix, but inserted after the registered name rather than before (USA).

Supreme an annual show run by the GCCF, where the BIS adult and BIS neuter are awarded the title of supreme CH/PR and supreme GR CH/GR PR, depending on their previous awards. These titles are held for life (UK).

TICA The Independent Cat Association (USA).

ticking the mottled coat pattern of certain breeds including Abyssinian.

tipped where the tip of the hair is a different colour from the root.

tom an entire male cat.

transfer the transfer of ownership of a pedigree cat. A kitten will be registered in the name of the breeder, but if the new owner wishes to show or breed from the kitten, ownership must be transferred into the new owner's name.

type the outward appearance of the cat, concerning mainly the skeletal and muscular structure. Each breed has certain standards regarding size, shape and length of body, head, nose, legs and tail.

undershot the opposite of overshot. This is where the lower jawline protrudes further out than the upper one.

VHC very highly commended – an award often given at a cat show to the cat placed after the first four winners.

wedge a term used to describe the shape of the muzzle of a cat.

whip tail a very long thin tail that, in some breeds, such as the Siamese, is the required standard, but in others would be considered a bad fault.

Wedge: a Foreign Black shows how it looks

LONGHAIRED BREEDS (PERSIANS)

Cats with long fur were recorded as long ago as the sixteenth century, when they were first imported into Europe. The original longhairs were found in Angora (now Ankara) in Turkey, and so were called 'Angoras'; a few years later some were found in Persia and as these had longer fur and a generally larger, wider body frame, they tended to be more popular. The two types were selectively bred together, and this was the beginning of the breed that we now call the Persian or Longhair.

These early longhairs looked quite different from those that currently grace our show benches; they were much longer in the face, and did not have the length or volume of coat that the judges look for today. The first record of a longhair in the UK was of a brown tabby in the mid 1880s, followed a few years later by a black in 1859. By the beginning of the twentieth century, thirteen different colours of Persian were recognised in the UK, including what must surely be one of the most beautiful breeds known, the Chinchilla.

Today, there are nearer fifty different colours and varieties within the Longhaired section and this is due, mainly, to the breeders, who have outcrossed with other breeds to produce these new colours. Perhaps the most spectacular of these newer varieties is the Colourpoint (USA Himalayan), where Siamese has been introduced to the breeding programme, resulting in a cat of true Persian type and with long fur, but with the restricted Siamese coat patterning. This is a most glamorous breed indeed, and is available in just as many different colours as the Siamese!

Type
In general, Longhaired cats should conform to the same standard of points, the coloration being the only difference but, as in all things, there are exceptions to the rule! These are, namely, the Chinchilla, Birman and Turkish Van, but there are also the longhaired varieties of Shorthairs, such as Balinese and Somalis, as well as the shorthaired version of the Longhair, by way of the Exotic Shorthair. Confused?

As a generalisation, Longhairs are probably the most glamorous and beautiful breed within the cat fancy, but they do require more than a modicum of attention to grooming, because of their long fur. The coat should be long and luxuriant, with a most definite ruff around the neck, and a brush-like tail.

In general, they are a small, stocky and elegant breed with large expressive eyes, short, small noses and little ears. Each variety calls for slight modifications to this basic standard, so do please read on if you think that you would like to own one of these lovely breeds.

Character and Temperament
This, again, has to be a generalisation, as the temperament can vary considerably between those breeds that are considered to be Longhaired, so do please read the breed notes for each variety before making a decision! This said, their good and bad points could generally be summed up as follows.

Good Points
They are a most beautiful, graceful and elegant breed, affectionate and loving, undemanding, and good with children. They generally have quiet voices, and are very docile and unlikely to want to fight.

Within reason, they do not mind being left alone while you are out at work, and are quite adaptable to living in a flat without outdoor access.

Bad Points
They require frequent, daily grooming (in most varieties), and will tend to shed their long fur over your furniture and carpets.

BI-COLOUR

As the name suggests, these are cats with a two-tone coat, one colour of which must be white and the other either black, blue, red or cream. Whatever the colour, the eyes should be a deep copper-gold. They should conform to the general standards for Longhairs and the only special consideration is that they will need to be bathed occasionally to keep their white parts sparkling.

White Longhair father with Pewter offspring

Bi-colour Longhair

BIRMAN

The Birman is definitely a 'breed' of longhaired cat, as opposed to a Longhaired variety like most cats in this section, and it has its own, quite different standard of points. It has most distinctive coat markings which are attributed to a quite delightful legend! The Birman was regarded as a sacred cat in Burma, and its duty was to guard the Burmese temples. One day, as the high priest lay dying, the cat walked over to him and, as it gently walked over the priest's frail body, the tips of its feet turned to brilliant white!

It is also thought that whenever a Birman cat dies, the soul of a priest accompanies it to Heaven. Charming as these stories are, the more likely truth is that this breed developed as a result of a Siamese crossing with a Bi-colour Longhair in France, where they were first seen in the early 1920s. Their popularity increased over the years. By 1959 they had been imported into the USA, and in the mid-1960s, were established in the UK.

The show standards require the Birman to be a medium-sized cat, with a long silky coat. The coat colour should be a pale even colour, with the darker points confined to the face, ears, tail and legs, with distinctive brown legs and white paw markings which must be symmetrical. The front legs should show white 'gloves', ending in a straight line over the paws, whilst the hind legs should show white 'gauntlets' that cover the top of the paw, and extend up the back of the leg to just below the hock. The eyes should be a bright sapphire blue.

There are currently two colours of Birman with championship status in the UK, namely Seal and Blue; the coat colour for the Seal should be an even pale creamy beige, with dark seal points, while the Blue should be a cool, bluish-white with slate grey points. For both varieties the paw pads should be pink with the nose leather being seal brown in the seal point, and slate grey in the blue point. More recently, provisional status has been granted in the UK to Chocolate, Lilac and Red Birmans.

Good Points
They are intelligent and clever, but not as naughty as Burmese and Siamese! They are gentle and loving, and, in general, have quiet voices. They are very sociable and good with other animals and children. They are (relatively) undemanding,

The Birman has a fine coat texture that does not tend to mat easily.

Birman

Bad Points
The Birman will require daily grooming to remove loose fur and scurf. It does not like to be confined, and will want to be part of the family.

BLACK

This is one of the oldest varieties of Longhair, and is most attractive with its luxuriant jet black fur and deep copper eyes. When adult, the Black Longhair should have a solid black coat with no trace of rustiness or white hairs. Do bear in mind, when viewing kittens of this variety, that they take time to develop true colour and density of coat and may appear paler than the adult until at least six months old.

Blue Longhair

BLUE CREAM

This is almost always a female-only variety, as with any tortie, and it is unlikely that any male with this colour of coat will prove to be fertile. Blue Creams are the result of mating Blue and Cream Longhairs together and, in the UK, there should be a well-mingled coat without any obvious patches of solid colour. The reverse is the standard in the USA, where definite, clearly separated areas of colour are preferred. The eyes should be a deep copper or orange in colour.

Black Longhair

BLUE

The Blue Longhair is one of the most popular colours for this breed, and also one of the oldest: it is said that this was Queen Victoria's favourite breed of cat! The coat should be thick and long, and the colour a pale, even, blue-grey with no shading or markings. The eye colour should be deep copper or orange.

Blue Cream Longhair

CAMEO

This variety is closely related to the Chinchilla and the Smoke, both of which have a 'tipped' coat. The Cameos can have this tipping in three different colours, Red, Cream and Tortie. There are also three densities of coloration: Shell, Shaded and Smoke, the latter being the only acceptable colour for a Tortie Cameo. This gives a total of seven different possible colours!

Shell Cameos have just a hint of colour at the tip of each hair strand, with the main length of the fur being white. In Shaded Cameos, the amount of tipping goes further down the hair strand, and in Smoke Cameos the white parts can only be seen when the fur is moved, or when the cat is walking. The eye colour should be copper.

CHINCHILLA

The Chinchilla, with its pure white coat, lightly tipped with black, has an almost ethereal and fairy-like look and it is not surprising that this breed is often seen in films, advertisements and on television. However, for all its glamour and dainty appearance, it is quite a strong and healthy breed and one of the most popular.

In general, the show standards require that the long white coat should be evenly tipped with black on the head, back, legs, tail and flanks. The chin, stomach and chest areas should be pure white. The nose leather should be brick red, outlined in black and the paw pads black. The eyes, which should be large and expressive, should be green or blue green in colour, with the eyelids outlined in black to give

Red Shaded Cameo

Chocolate Longhair

the impression of a line of 'mascara'.

In the USA, the Chinchilla should conform to the general type for Persians, whereas in the UK this breed is generally more lightly boned than the other Longhairs, and tends to have a slightly longer muzzle.

In temperament, it is very much the same as the other varieties of Longhair, being gentle, placid, loving and affectionate, but possibly a little more inquisitive. Its only drawback is that the soft white coat does tend to shed and, being white, is more noticeable on furniture! It may also be necessary to bath a Chinchilla more frequently to keep the coat clean and sparkling.

CHOCOLATE

The Self Chocolate is one of the newer colours and, like the Self Lilac, is a 'by-product' of the Colour-point breeding programme. The general type should be that of the Longhair, with a coat of a solid, even, medium chocolate brown colour, with matching nose leather and paw pads, and deep copper eyes.

Chinchilla

Tortie-tabby Point Colourpoint (Himalayan in USA)

COLOURPOINT
(USA Himalayan)

The Colourpoint is most definitely a man-made breed, 'manufactured' by dedicated breeders over a period of many years. Sometimes confused with both Birmans and Balinese, it is a breed of quite obvious Longhaired type, but with the restricted Siamese coat patterning.

Colourpoints have been the result of mating Blue or Black Longhairs with Siamese, and the early progeny did have much longer, 'Siamesy' faces. Careful and selective breeding has resulted not only in the fact that Colourpoints are now some of the 'typiest' Longhairs seen currently on the show bench, but that they are also now available in a wide variety of colours – at the time of writing there are twenty acceptable coat colours in the UK! Whatever the colour, the points must be restricted to the same areas as in the Siamese, namely the face, ears, tail and legs, with the eyes a deep, vivid blue in colour.

The main colour variations of the Colourpoint are as follows:

Seal Point creamy-beige on the main body, with dark seal brown points, and the same dark seal brown colouring for the nose leather and paw pads.

Blue Point glacial white on the main body, with slate blue points, and the same colour for the nose leather and paw pads.

Chocolate Point pale ivory on the main body, warm milk chocolate points, with pinkish nose leather and paw pads.

Lilac Point glacial white on the main body, with pinky-blue points, and lavender pink paw pads and nose leather.

Red Point creamy-white on the main body, with orangey red points, and deep flesh-pink paw pads and nose leather.

Cream Point pale creamy white on the main body, with darker cream on the points, and flesh pink nose leather and paw pads.

Tortie Point (Seal, Blue, Chocolate and Lilac) these should have the body colour that corresponds to that recommended for the solid-point variety, and should be well mingled with red and cream in the Seal Tortie and cream in the other colours.

Tabby Point (Seal, Blue, Chocolate, Lilac, Red and Cream) the body colour should again correspond to that of the solid-point colour, with the points showing tabby markings and with a distinctive 'M' marking on the forehead.

Cream Point Colourpoint (Himalayan in USA)

Cream Longhair

Lilac Longhair

CREAM

Although the Cream Longhair has been in existence since the end of the last century, it was not considered very popular and was usually regarded as a poor-coloured red because of its pale hue. Today, the reverse is true, and the Cream is admired for its pale colour, which should never be too 'hot', and which is shown off well by the contrasting deep copper-coloured eyes.

GOLDEN and SHADED GOLDEN

These are a new breed that have only been seen in recent years, and resulted when two Chinchillas, that carry a recessive 'red' gene, were mated together. The Golden Persian should have typical Longhair type, and be heavier and shorter-faced than the Chinchilla. The coat should display the same amount of tipping seen in the Chinchilla, but the colour must be a basic rich cream colour lightly tipped with brown and shading to a lighter hue on the underparts and chin.

The Shaded Golden should appear the same, but with much denser tipping, similar to that seen in the Shaded Silver (another close relative). With either variety, the eyes should be a delightful bright green.

LILAC

As with the Self Chocolate, the Lilac has arrived by way of the Colourpoint breeding programme, but should still conform to the general Longhair type. With this variety, the coat should be a solid pinky dove-grey right through the fur, from tip to root, and should not have any masking, or patches of lighter or darker fur. The eyes should be copper or orange.

Golden Longhair (left) and Shaded Golden Longhair (right)

Pewter

PEWTER

This breed is quite similar to the Chinchilla, but has a much more heavily tipped coat, and is the result of mating any of the self-coloured Longhairs with the Chinchilla. In all other ways, the Pewter should conform to the general Longhair standard of points and have deep copper or orange-coloured eyes.

RED

Although this is one of the older colours of Longhair, it is not easy to breed one that is clear-coated and without tabby markings. The coat should be a clear, rich orange colour, the eyes deep copper, and the nose leather and paw pads brick red.

SHADED SILVER

This is another breed that is closely linked with the Chinchilla. It is, however, more heavily tipped, although not so strongly as in the Pewter. In some countries this is a recognised breed, but in the UK it does not yet have championship status. Shaded Silvers conform to the Chinchilla standards, having a similar shape, green (or blue green) eyes, the same well-marked nose leather and a distinctive 'mascara' look around their eyes.

Shaded Silver

Red Longhair

Red Tabby Longhair

SMOKE

Currently recognised in the UK, in two colour varieties, the Black Smoke and the Blue Smoke, these are another most attractive Longhaired variety. The Smoke was originally bred by crossing a Chinchilla with a Black Longhair, and was first seen at a British cat show as far back as 1870. The tipping on a Smoke is almost literally the reverse of that seen on a Chinchilla.

With the Smoke, only the very base of the coat should be white, with the tipped effect taking up the majority of the length of the fur.

In the Black variety, the coat should appear black until the fur is ruffled to expose the white base. With the Blue, the same should be true, but here there is a slate grey mantle overlying the white. In either colour, the type should be typical of the Longhair breed, and the eyes should be a deep copper or orange in colour.

TABBY

These are probably the oldest known variety of Longhair, and are still popular, but not as much as some of the more glamorous newer varieties. The original Brown Tabby is only occasionally seen on the show bench today, as is the newer Red Tabby, whereas the Silver Tabby is rapidly becoming more popular and is greatly sought after.

The Tabby, of whichever colour, should be very much of the basic Longhair type, with a massive coat that often makes it difficult to discern the exact markings, which may be either classic or mackerel. The eye colour in the Brown and Red Tabbies should be copper, or deep orange, but in the Silver Tabby it is required to be green or hazel.

Brown Tabby Longhair

Smoke Longhair

White Longhair: Blue-eyed

White Longhair: Odd-eyed

White Longhair: Orange-eyed

WHITE

This is one of the oldest colour varieties in the Longhaired section and most of the original Angoras were white. The Whites seen today have been selectively bred over many, many generations and now conform to the type for the Persian Longhair, with the typical short face and small neat ears. There are three acceptable eye colours for this breed, Orange Eyed (deep orange or copper), Blue Eyed (deep, bright blue) and Odd Eyed (one blue and one orange eye). The only extra consideration needed with a White Longhair is that of extra bathing, as the coat can get dirty very easily, especially if the cat has access to the garden

EXOTIC SHORTHAIRS

In the UK these are classified under the Longhaired section as 'AV SH of Persian Type', which is exactly what this breed is – a shorthaired Longhair! In all ways, they should conform to the standard of points set out for Longhaired varieties, the only difference being that they have a short, plush coat. This is another man-made variety, and is basically a cross between a Longhair and a British Shorthair, and so has the short coat, but with the typical short face of the Longhair. They are bred in almost all the colours available for their Longhaired cousins, and are becoming rapidly more popular, although only bred in the UK for a few years.

Blue Exotic Shorthair

Tortie and White Longhair (Calico in the USA)

TORTOISESHELL

This is, most usually, a female-only variety and any males born are most often found to be sterile. This is a difficult variety to breed and, for this reason, they are relatively scarce. The coat colour should have a patched selection of red, cream and black and the type should be typically Longhaired, with deep copper or orange eyes.

TORTIE and WHITE (USA Calico)

This variety is very much the same as the Tortoiseshell, but should have solid white patches intermingled with the tortie markings.

Tortoiseshell Longhair

TURKISH (USA Turkish Van/ Swimming Cat)

The general belief is that cats hate water, and this breed is the exception to prove the rule – it loves water, and even likes to go for a swim! Although the Turkish is classified as a Longhair in the UK, it is quite dissimilar in appearance and type to the general standards for the Longhairs; just like the Birman, it is a breed in its own right.

The Turkish has a longer nose, a wedge-shaped face and larger ears. The coat pattern is a basic white, interspaced with auburn markings on the head, ears and tail. The coat is not as long as is seen in most Persians and, during the summer months, tends to moult quite drastically. The Turkish should have a good brush-like tail but may, in some seasons, have little by way of a very noticeable neck ruff.

Good Points
It is intelligent and certainly different! A strong, sturdy breed, it likes to play with water, and also to swim!

Bad Points
Of course, you may not want a cat that likes to share your bathtime with you! It does need regular grooming, and tends to shed fur in the spring more than other Longhairs.

Turkish (Turkish Van or Swimming Cat in USA)

BRITISH SHORTHAIRS

The British Shorthairs are the native cat of Britain, and have long been very popular as they are tough, robust and strong with a delightfully gentle disposition. Their history goes back many centuries, probably to Roman times, and it is thought that invading Roman troops first brought cats to the British Isles. Although records of the cat fancy have only been in existence for the last 100 years or so, it is clear from old paintings that shorthaired cats, similar to the modern British Shorthair, have been around for many, many years!

It is thought that they were originally kept for their mousing ability and this is probably the main reason for their early popularity. When early immigrants left the UK for America, these cats were taken along as mousers. It was not long before they started breeding, often with cats brought to America from other parts of the world, and this gave rise to a similar breed now known as the American Shorthair.

The first Shorthairs were tabbies, one of the oldest known coat patterns seen in cats. It is likely that they descended from the European wildcat, whose tabby patterning acted as a camouflage, protecting it from attack by predators. Cats with tabby stripes or spots were certainly known in ancient Egypt, as such cats were frequently featured in drawings and paintings. Brown Spotted Tabby Shorthairs were amongst the first cats to be shown, but over the years their popularity seems to have decreased, with the more glamorous Silver Tabbies taking over in the popularity stakes.

British Shorthairs are available today in a variety of coat colours and patterns, many of which are the result of selective breeding with Longhairs to introduce these new variations. Two recent examples are the British Shorthair Colourpoint, with its striking restricted coat pattern, and the British Shorthair Silver Tipped, which has a white coat tipped with black like the Chinchilla.

Type

British Shorthairs are larger than most other varieties, and should be strong, sturdy and muscular, with the males tending to be bigger than the females. The chest should be deep and broad, with short strong legs, and neat, rounded paws. The head should be wide and well rounded, particularly in the males, who should have a definite 'jowled' look. The ears should be small, neat and set well apart, and the nose short and wide. The coat is short and dense, but without being 'woolly'.

The eyes are large, round and lustrous: the colour should be a deep copper or orange, except in Silver Tabbies and Silver Tipped (green), Colourpoints (blue), White (orange, blue or odd-eyed) and Manx (orange, blue or odd-eyed). The tail should be short, thick at the base of the spine, and tapering to a rounded tip, except in the Manx varieties, where the tail should be completely absent.

In general, the British Shorthair should appear to be a big, strong cat with a definite chunky, cobby look about it; although the Silver Tabbies, Silver Tipped and Manx do tend to be rather less chunky.

Character and Temperament

Gentle giants is probably an apt description as a generalisation! They are a delightful breed, loving and affectionate and not particularly demanding. Their short, plushy coats require only a weekly brush to remove the dead fur and prevent mats forming, although the Black will benefit from an occasional 'polish' with a chamois leather to keep its coat gleaming! Their voices are quiet, and they do not mind being left alone if you have to go out to work.

Bi-colour Shorthair

Black Shorthair

They also tend to have less wanderlust than many other breeds, and seem content to live in a flat or apartment. They tend to enjoy robust good health, and are unlikely to become faddy eaters – British cats do like their food!

Good Points

They are gentle-natured and affectionate, quiet in voice, and they like other animals and children. They need little grooming, do not mind being confined or left alone and are, generally, a healthy, sturdy breed.

Bad Points

British Shorthairs arrive as cute, cuddly kittens that will develop into large cats; some people prefer a more dainty feline, so make sure you see the adult version before you buy!

They do love their food, and so are more prone to becoming overweight than other breeds. A healthy appetite is one thing, but obesity does put a great strain on the heart!

BI-COLOUR

As the name suggests, this is a two-tone cat that can be any of the recognised British colours, but with white patching; preferably, the underparts should be white with symmetrical patches of solid colour on the main body.

BLACK

Black cats seem to have gone both in and out of favour during history: at worst, they were thought to be witches' familiars and, at best, a symbol of good fortune! Cats are often thought of as being rather perverse creatures, but humans can be just the same! Today, the Blacks are a most popular colour, with their jet black, glossy coats set off by deep copper-coloured eyes. Show standards require the coat to be a solid black from tip to root, with no trace of rustiness, white hairs or vestigial tabby markings. (Younger kittens may appear slightly rusty, so do not be put off buying one of these, as it will most likely grow up to be a deep, solid black.) The nose leather and paw pads should be a true jet black.

BLUE

This is probably the most popular colour of British Shorthair, and certainly one of the more commonly known. It is a most striking cat, large and muscular, with a blue-grey coat that has a definite 'plushy' texture, and deep copper-coloured eyes. In Europe, this colour is known as Chartreux or Chartreuse, and it is a somewhat controversial point as to whether these cats are all the same breed, but with a different name, or if they are, indeed, two quite different varieties!

Blue Shorthair

Blue Cream Shorthair

Blue and Tortie Point Colourpoint Shorthair

BLUE CREAM

The standard for any breed with a tortoiseshell patterning varies between the UK and the USA; the British standards require the coat to be well mingled, while the American call for a cat that has quite obvious patches of different colours. Whichever standard is followed, the coat colour should be a mixture of blue and cream without any white patches, or hairs, and the eyes should be deep copper. As with any tortie, this is invariably a female-only variety, and if a rare male kitten is born, it is infertile in most cases.

COLOURPOINT

This is a relative newcomer to the British scene, and is the result of crossing the British with the Longhair Colourpoint. For the first few generations, the coats were somewhat more fluffy than most British cats, due to the introduction of the Longhair gene, but, with selective breeding, this is no longer the case, and the British Shorthaired Colourpoints have now been recognised by the GCCF. The coat pattern, as with any Colourpoint, should be restricted to the face, ears, legs and tail, with the main body colour a pale cream in the brown tones, and glacial white in the blue tones.

Cream Shorthair

CREAM

This is a rarer colour of British Shorthair, and one that is not easy to breed; the standard calls for an even, pale cream-coloured coat, without any tabby 'ghost' markings, but in practice this is most difficult to achieve. The paw pads and nose leather should be pink.

105

MANX

Although tailless cats are found in many parts of the world, the Manx is probably the best-known variety, and comes from the Isle of Man. It is thought that sailors first brought tailless cats to the island from the Far East, and records dating back 200 years confirm that tailless cats were in existence on the island at that time. The Isle of Man is geographically, and politically, remote from the mainland of Great Britain and so, with the lack of other cats to breed with, the tailless variety became indigenous. Manx cats have always been considered a symbol of good fortune, and their image is used on the Manx currency.

The show standard for the Manx breed is quite different from the other British Shorthairs, and calls for a complete absence of tail with a small dip in the base of the spine where the tail would have been; if there is any vestige of a tail, the cat is called a 'stumpy', and these are not suitable for the show bench.

The back is shorter than in most cats, with the back legs longer than the front ones, giving the cat a characteristic 'rabbity' look. The coat should be short and glossy, with a thick undercoat, and may be of any colour. The eye colour should be in sympathy with the coat colour, with white Manx having blue, orange or odd eyes. The head shape is generally quite similar to that of the other British

breeds, but the nose is slightly longer, and with no obvious nose break.

Good Points
The Manx is a rare breed that will prove quite a conversation piece. It is affectionate and gentle, good with other animals and children, and quiet in voice.

Bad Points
The thick undercoat will need daily grooming to prevent mats forming.

SMOKE

This is the result of early attempts by breeders to introduce new coat colours and patterns into the British Shorthair cats, and was first seen at the end of the last century. The first Smokes were produced by crossing a Shorthair Silver Tabby with a Longhair Smoke, and mating the progeny back to British Blues to keep the coat suitably short.

By doing this, the blue gene was introduced and, today, a Smoke can be either black or blue, although the colour should be of the same hue that is recommended for the solid colours. At first sight, a Smoke does appear to be a solid colour, and it is only when the cat moves, or the fur is ruffled, that the white undercoat is revealed. As with most Shorthair cats, the eye colour should be deep orange or copper.

Manx

Smoke Shorthair

Silver Tabby Shorthairs

TABBY and SPOTTED TABBY

There are two main types of this variety, the Tabby and the Spotted Tabby, each of which is recognised in three different colours, Red, Brown or Silver. The general standards require the cat to be of overall British type, but the Silvers may be slightly lighter in weight. Whichever coat pattern the cat has, the markings should be clearly defined stripes or spots of a darker colour set off against a lighter body coat colour, with the Tabby showing a classic 'M' marking on the forehead.

In the Red, the coat should be a rich red, with the markings a deeper red; the nose leather and paw pads should be brick red, and the eye colour deep orange or copper.

The Brown should have a sable brown background colour, with the markings in black; the nose leather should be brick red, the paw pads black and the eyes orange.

The Silver Tabbies have a clear, silver body colour with the markings in black; the nose leather may be brick red or black, with black paw pads, and green or hazel eyes.

Silver Spotted Tabby Shorthair

Red Spotted Tabby Shorthair

TIPPED

This is one of the newer varieties and was originally developed by mating a Silver Tabby with a Chinchilla Longhair. This gave rise to a shorthaired cat, with the distinctive Chinchilla 'tipping'.

The coat colour should be pure white, with black tips along the back, head, ears, tail, legs and flanks, with the underparts pure white, and the eyes should be green. As with the Chinchilla, the nose leather should be brick red, outlined in black, the paw pads black, and the eyes outlined in black, giving a 'mascara' effect.

Through various breeding programmes, the Tipped is now seen in a wide variety of colours, and these require the eyes to be a deep orange. In all respects, the tipping should be of the same density as seen in the Silver.

Silver Tipped Shorthair

White Shorthair: Orange-eyed

TORTOISESHELL and TORTIE and WHITE

The Tortie is a colourful cat, whose coat colour is a mixture of red, cream and black. A female-only variety, Torties are produced by mating a Tortie female to a solid red, cream or black male cat. The main body colour should be well mingled, with no white hairs, with evenly distributed patches of colour on the face and legs, and, preferably, a red blaze down the centre of the face.

By mating a Tortie to a Bi-colour, it is possible to produce a Tortie and White. In this variety the coat should be made up of evenly distributed patches of colour, the underparts being white. The cat should have a white facial blaze.

In both cases, the eyes should be deep copper or orange.

WHITE

Shorthaired whites should have a completely white coat with no trace of any markings or 'yellowing'. As with the white Longhairs, the eye colour can be orange, blue or odd-eyed, with one eye of either colour. The paw pads and nose leather should always be pink. The only extra consideration to be taken into account with this colour is that it will need bathing more frequently, especially if allowed out!

Tortoiseshell Shorthair

FOREIGN SHORTHAIRS

Many different breeds fall into the general category of Foreign Shorthairs, each of which have their own particular charm, appeal, character and standard.

Some of the Foreign Shorthairs are the result of natural mutation, as seen in the curly-coated Devon and Cornish Rex, while others, such as the Korat, were imported from abroad. Several man-made varieties are also available, these being the results of out-crossing with other breeds, and producing striking-looking cats such as the Oriental Spotted Tabby.

As each of these is a breed in its own right, they must be considered separately.

ABYSSINIAN and SOMALI

History
Abyssinian cats were first seen in the UK in the mid 1800s, and are thought to have been imported from Abyssinia. Legend has it that they were the direct descendants of the sacred cats of Egypt, and their markings certainly look similar to those seen in ancient Egyptian drawings of cats. Whether this is fact or a romantic myth is left to the imagination!

Over the years, an occasional longhaired mutant kitten appeared in litters, and these were generally ignored. It is only in recent years that they have been recognised as a breed and have been given the name Somali.

Type
The Abyssinian is a medium-sized cat that should feel firm and muscular. It has a most distinctive ticked coat, which gives it an almost 'wild cat' appearance that is most attractive.

The coat texture should be short, fine, close-lying and lustrous. The head should be a rounded wedge-shape, with large, wide-set ears, tufted at the tips, and the neck should appear long and elegant. Three main colours are recognised in this breed.

Ruddy (or Usual) is a ruddy, reddish brown, ticked in black, with black paw pads, brick red nose leather, and green or hazel eyes.

Sorrel (or Red) is a deep rich copper red, ticked with a darker red or chocolate brown. The nose leather and paw pads are pink and the eyes are green or hazel.

Blue is a blue-grey coat ticked with dark steel blue. This cat has a deep pink nose leather and mauve pink paw pads.

Newer colour variations, such as Lilac, Chocolate and Silver, have been introduced by selective breeding, but these are still awaiting official recognition.

The Somali is available in the same colour variations as the Abyssinian, and should conform to the same general standards; the only difference being

Normal Abyssinian

that the coat should be medium long and with a distinctive, foxy, brush-like tail.

Character and Temperament
Both Abyssinians and Somalis have outgoing personalities and are highly intelligent. Although their coat colouring gives them a wild-cat appearance, there is nothing very wild about their temperament, as they are a gentle and loving breed. They are very active and love playing games, but do not like to be confined or left on their own.

Good Points
Their short, close-lying fur needs little by way of special grooming; a weekly brush, and a polish with a chamois leather will keep them glowing. They are most attractive in appearance. They have a gentle and loving temperament, are good with children, and are intelligent.

Bad Points
The Somali will require more regular grooming, especially around the neck ruff and the brush-like tail. Abyssinians and Somalis do not like to be confined, and so are not really suitable for flat dwellers. These cats like freedom and should have access to a garden. They do not like to be left alone.

Red Abyssinian

Blue Abyssinians

CORNISH REX

History

This distinctive breed, with its close-lying curly coat, was first seen in a litter of Cornish farm kittens in 1950: only one kitten had a curly coat, while all its siblings had normal straight fur. The owner was somewhat confused by this and, after consulting her vet, decided that when the little tom kitten grew up it should be mated back to its mother.

The result was several kittens in the litter with the same curly coats, and so a breeding programme was begun to continue this variation. The first Cornish Rexes had a very 'moggy' appearance; it was only their curious curly coat that made them appear different from the other farm cats. The breeding programmes used to continue this line incorporated the use of cats of a more 'foreign' type, and the Cornish Rex today should have a definite 'foreign' look about it.

Type

The general body should have a long, elegant appearance, but still feel firm and muscular, with long legs and a long, whip-like tail. The head is wedge-shaped, with a long, straight nose, large, wide-set ears and oval-shaped eyes. The coat should be well rexed all over, with short curly fur showing a 'rip-pled' effect; a shaggy coat, or any un-rexed patches, are considered a fault, and the whiskers and eyebrows should be curly too.

Cornish Rex can have almost any coat colour or pattern, the most important point being that the coat is well rexed. The eye colour should be in keeping with the coat colour.

Character and Temperament

This is a lively, intelligent and active breed that needs little grooming and makes an ideal pet for the whole family. Although the coat is very short, the Cornish Rex is a hardy cat and does not need extra heating, over and above the normal household environment.

Good Points

The Cornish Rex is a very different cat, with curly fur. It is intelligent and outgoing, easy to groom and look after, and it loves people and children. Rex fur tends to be non-allergenic, and so this is often the only breed that asthmatic cat lovers can tolerate. It does not mind being trained to a collar and lead.

Bad Points

The Cornish Rex does like attention, and will not be happy left on its own. It likes its food and can tend towards obesity if the diet is not closely monitored.

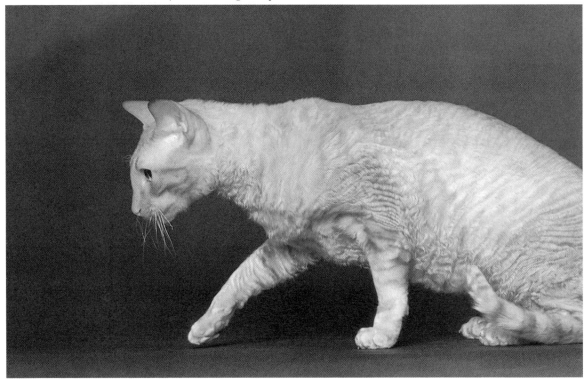

Red Cornish Rex

Tortoiseshell Devon Rex

DEVON REX

History
This is another curly-coated breed, which was first noticed in Devon in 1960. At the time, it was thought that this was the result of the same mutation that produced the Cornish Rex, but when the two were mated together, all the kittens were straight-coated, and it was then realised that the Devon Rex was a quite distinct breed with a different genetic composition.

Type
The most commonly used description of a Devon Rex is that it has a pixie-like face, and this is quite true. Other, less flattering, descriptions refer to this breed as looking like ET! It is most certainly an unusual-looking cat, with a small face, large lustrous eyes, and huge ears – perhaps not everyone's taste in felines!

The head shape should be generally rounded, but with a flat top, rounded cheeks, a definite nose break in profile, and with large low-set ears. The body is medium to small in size, with a broad chest, long slim legs and a long neck. The tail is long, thin and covered in downy fur.

As with the Cornish Rex, the Devon may be of almost any coat colour or pattern. However, as the coat is shorter, it can, at times, look somewhat bald.

Character and Temperament
The pixie-like expression of this breed is the outward manifestation of a most definitely impish character! The Devons may not seem beautiful in everyone's eyes, but they are a breed with an obvious sense of humour and those who love them could not bear to be without one of these enchanting little cats!

Good Points
This cat is a conversation piece: Devon Rex look like no other breed! They are loving, affectionate and good natured. They love people and all the attention that can be offered. The Devon Rex is intelligent. It is easy to groom, but do not overdo it, as they do not have a lot of fur. They should be brushed gently, and *never* with a metal comb. They are very playful, with outgoing personalities. They do not usually cause an allergic reaction in asthma sufferers.

Korat

Bad Points
They do not like to be left alone. You will need to watch their weight, as they are prone to over-eating!

KORAT

History
The Korat is a very old breed, originating from Thailand, and its history can be traced back hundreds of years. It was not until this century that they were imported to the west, first to America in the early 1950s, and from there to the UK in 1972. In Thailand, they are known as *Si-Siwat* which, translated, means 'good fortune', and in their native country they are highly prized.

The Korat, today, is one of the few 'pure' breeds as no other type of cat has been used in its breeding programmes; it is only available in one colour, silver blue, and although it is very popular in America, it is still a comparatively rare breed in the UK at the time of writing.

Type
Some of the most striking features of the Korat are its heart-shaped face, large green eyes and typically sweet expression. The top of the head should be flat, with a gently pointed muzzle, and with medium-sized ears set high on the head. In profile, the nose should show a slight break. The eyes are large, round and, in adulthood, should be a brilliant green, although kittens' eyes tend to have a slight yellow tinge. The body is of medium size, and should be muscular and firm, with the back being slightly rounded. The coat is short, sleek and close-lying, and is an even silvery blue all over, with no white hairs or patches. The nose leather and paw pads should be blue or lavender.

Character and Temperament
The Korat is a quiet, gentle and loving little cat with a delightful disposition. It is an intelligent breed and its placid nature makes it an ideal companion for someone who shares a similar outlook on life. Korats do not like loud noises, bangs and thumps, or over-active and unruly children!

Good Points
The Korat is sweet, loving and gentle. It is a very pretty breed that is still quite rare. It is quiet in voice – except when calling! The Korat is intelligent, but undemanding, good with other animals, and adapts well to life in a flat.

Bad Points
It is not really suitable for a loud, noisy household!

ORIENTAL and ANGORA

History
The Orientals, or Foreigns, are really Siamese-shaped cats, but without the restricted coat patterning. They were developed by mating Siamese with British or American (Domestic) Shorthairs to introduce new colours, which can be solid, Tabby or Tortie. The first colour to be purposely bred was a medium brown, called the Havana, as its colour resembled a Havana cigar. This was back in the early 1950s, and today the Oriental is recognised in the UK in eight basic colours and patterns; Havana, White, Black, Blue, Lilac, Tortie, Spotted Tabby and Classic Tabby, although there are a myriad other colours, as yet unrecognised, that are the results of more experimental breeding.

The Angora, in the UK, is a recently recognised breed. It is, to all intents and purposes, a Longhaired Oriental, and is thus classified under the Foreign Shorthaired section. It should not, however, be confused with the Turkish Angora, which is a breed recognised in the USA, which was actually imported from Ankara in Turkey.

Type
The general shape should be that of a Siamese, with a long, slim and lithe body, long legs, and a long whip-like tail. The head shape should be a long wedge, with a flat skull and large ears set wide apart, and in profile should show a long straight nose without a break. The eyes should be almond-shaped, with the typical oriental slant, and without a squint.

The coat and eye colours should be as follows:
Havana is a rich warm chestnut brown, solid to the root, without any white hairs. The paw pads should be pinky brown, the nose leather brown, and the eyes bright green.
White is a pure white with no black hairs or shading of any hue. The nose leather should be pale pink, the paw pads a slightly darker pink, and eyes brilliant sapphire blue.
Black should be jet black all over, solid to the roots and without any white hairs. The nose leather and paw pads should be black, and the eyes a brilliant green.
Blue is a light, medium blue colour, solid to the root. The nose leather and paw pads should be blue, and the eyes green.
Lilac is a pinkish frosty grey. The nose leather and paw pads are lavender and the eyes are green.
Tortie is a well-mingled mixture of red, cream and brown, with a facial blaze. The nose leather and paw pads should be black and/or pink, and the eyes green.

Foreign Black (Oriental Black)

In the **Spotted Tabby**, the body pattern should show clearly defined and symmetrical spotting. The nose leather and paw pads should be in keeping with the coat colour, and the eyes should be green.

In the **Classic Tabby**, the markings should be clearly defined stripes, with a characteristic 'M' mark on the forehead. The nose leather and paw pads should be in keeping with the coat colour, and the eyes should be green.

The **Angora** should conform to all the above standards, but have a medium long coat, with a noticeable neck ruff, and a brush-like tail.

Character and Temperament

The Orientals have very much the same character and temperament as their Siamese ancestors, and can be just as demanding! They are an active and intelligent breed, and are most elegant and aristocratic in appearance.

Good Points
This is an elegant and attractive breed. Their short fur requires little by way of special grooming. They are affectionate and playful, and make a most companionable breed.

Bad Points
They tend to have loud 'Siamese' voices, but less so if neutered. They are demanding – they like to have your attention as much as possible! They do not like to be left alone without either a human or feline companion. Angoras require regular grooming.

Lilac Oriental Spotted Tabby

RUSSIAN BLUE

History
It is thought that the Russian Blue was first brought to the UK by sailors, who had found this distinctive breed of cat in the Russian port of Archangel in the nineteenth century. Similar blue cats are known to exist in Russia and Scandinavia, so it is quite possible that this was its true origin.

Early breeding programmes used British Blue, or Blue Point Siamese, as out-crosses, as there were few pure Russians available in the UK. This, of course, caused them to lose their typical Russian look, and it has taken many generations of pure breeding in recent years to reinstate the breed true to type. Today, they are a popular breed and are frequently seen on the show bench.

Type
The Russian Blue is a medium to large, elegant cat, with a distinctive short, plushy coat of a blue grey colour that has a silvery sheen. The head is medium long, with large, pointed ears set straight and high up on the flat, narrow skull. In profile, there should be a change of angle just above the nose. The legs are long and give the Russian its characteristic graceful appearance. The eyes are almond-shaped and set wide apart, but slant towards the nose, and should be a bright, brilliant green in colour.

Character and Temperament
This breed is most quiet, gentle and loving, but does have a tendency towards shyness. It loves people, but does not like too much by way of noisy household hubbub and prefers a quiet environment. Russian Blues become very attached to their owners and are unlikely to wander; for this reason, it is another breed that is happy to live in a flat, and will not pine for the great outdoors!

Good Points
The Russian Blue is very sweet natured. It is easy to groom and care for. It is intelligent, companionable, and becomes devoted to its owner. It is quiet in voice and is happy to live its life indoors in a flat or apartment.

Bad Points
It does not like a noisy, busy home. Its voice is so quiet that it can be difficult to tell if a female is calling! It can be shy.

Russian Blue

BURMESE

History

Today, Burmese cats are probably the single most popular breed in the UK, but their history is really quite recent. It is thought that brown, shorthaired cats have existed in Burma and Thailand for several centuries and, like the Birman breed, the Burmese also lays claim to being the sacred cat of Burma with the responsibility of guarding the temples – but such is the way of legends and fables and, although there is probably no truth in the stories, it does give romantic appeal to this breed!

It was not until 1930 that one such female cat was brought from Burma and imported to the west coast of the USA. It was decided to mate her with a Seal Point Siamese, as this was the breed with the closest physical resemblance, and the progeny were Burmese/Siamese hybrids. However, when she was mated back to one of her sons, brown kittens just like herself were present in the litter, thus proving that this little brown cat was indeed a 'new' breed, and not a Siamese hybrid as was first thought.

Although not so obviously striking in appearance as the Siamese, the Burmese was found to have the most delightful character and personality, and a much quieter voice than the Siamese! For these reasons their popularity increased rapidly and, in 1948, the first examples of this breed were imported into the UK, where they were greatly admired.

In 1955, a great surprise occurred – in a litter of Burmese kittens, one appeared to be a silvery blue colour and this is now generally agreed to have been the first Blue Burmese. It was, most applicably, named Sealcoat Blue Surprise, and this was the beginning of a whole new generation of Burmese and their associated colours.

Chocolate and Lilac Burmese had been found in litters of American Burmese, and these were imported into the UK. After all, if it was possible to develop Red, Cream and Tortie Siamese, then why not Burmese too? A well-structured breeding programme was set up to produce these colours and, today, Burmese are available in ten different colours in the UK – Brown, Blue, Chocolate, Lilac, Red, Cream, Brown Tortie, Blue Tortie, Lilac Tortie and Chocolate Tortie. In the USA, generally, only the Brown (Sable), Blue, Chocolate (Champagne) and Lilac (Platinum) are recognised as Burmese, the other colours being known as Malayans.

Type

Whatever the coat colour, the Burmese type and shape should be the same. Burmese are medium-sized cats, with a strong and muscular feel about them. The head should show a well-rounded dome, both front-on and in profile, with wide-set, rounded ears, and a blunt wedge-like muzzle. The nose should show a definite nose break, and the chin should be firm and strong, and not receding.

The tail should be of a proportionate length to the body and, when held back, should just reach the shoulder; it should be thicker at the base, and gently taper to the end, with a typical 'paint-brush' tip and no tail fault. The eyes are of an oriental almond-shape, set well apart and should be of a chartreuse yellow colour.

The coat should be sleek, close-lying, showing a definite glossy sheen whatever the colour, and should never have any white hairs or patches. It is equally important to have a coat colour that is free from any barring or ghost tabby markings.

Character and Temperament

Burmese cats and kittens are gentle hooligans that are the 'Peter Pans' of the cat world – they just don't like to grow up, and can be as mischievous at ten years old as at ten weeks! They are, above all, very friendly towards people, but can be reservedly territorial towards unfamiliar cats and other animals.

They are extremely trusting, and afraid of little, so they can get themselves into all sorts of difficult situations. If your Burmese is to have free range, do make sure that it wears an identity tag with your name on it, not the cat's, as this trusting breed will treat everyone as a friend, especially if its name is called.

They do also like to explore and, again, this can result in disastrous consequences; they will try to get into your washing machine, drier and oven, amongst other appliances in your home, but, just as important, may also wander off to explore the outside world, and end up getting locked into an outside shed. They also have a penchant for cars and, in the summer when many car owners leave windows open, will happily curl up on the back seat for a snooze, end up hundreds of miles from home, and be unable to find their way back.

Just like the Siamese, they tend to be destructive if left on their own for any length of time, and for this reason it is unlikely that any responsible breeder will allow you to have a sole kitten if you are out at work all day and do not have some other feline or canine companion for a Burmese.

Good Points

This cat has personality plus! It is intelligent, attractive, very sweet natured, most companionable and will sense your moods and feelings. The Burmese loves people and children. It may be trained to a collar, harness or lead. It is very playful and amusing and needs little special grooming, other than a weekly brush to remove dead fur and skin debris.

Bad Points

The Burmese does not like to be left alone. It can be taxing and time consuming; Burmese think that they deserve prime consideration in your home! This breed likes to sleep in bed with its owners.

Its trusting nature can get it into situations it cannot get out of. It may wander and is more likely to get into road accidents than other breeds. It can be vociferous, especially if un-neutered, but not to the same extent as Siamese.

BROWN

This should be a deep sable brown, shading to a slightly lighter colour on the underparts. The nose leather and paw pads should be dark brown. Kittens may show slight, light tabby barring which may disappear when adult, so do not dismiss such a kitten when looking at a litter as a kitten marked in this way can still grow into a lovely cat with a perfect coat that can be shown successfully.

Brown Burmese

Blue Burmese

BLUE

This cat is a soft silver grey, shading to a slightly lighter colour on the underparts, but the coat should always have a 'silvery' tinge. The nose leather and paw pads should be grey.

CHOCOLATE

This is a warm milk chocolate colour, with as little by way of masking as possible, and shading to a slightly lighter colour on the underparts. The nose leather and paw pads should be chocolate brown.

Chocolate Burmese

Lilac Burmese

Red Burmese

LILAC

This is a pale dove grey with a pinky tinge – a 'cold' blue grey is a fault, but the colour may be a shade darker on the ears and tail. The nose leather and paw pads should be lavender pink.

RED

This is a rich tangerine that should not be too orange, with slightly darker ears and mask. The nose leather and paw pads should be most definitely pink.

Cream Burmese

Blue Tortie Burmese

Brown Tortie Burmese

CREAM

This cat should be a pale cream colour, with an obvious 'powdery' look around the head; it is a fault for a cream to appear in too 'hot' a colour. The nose leather and paw pads should be pink.

BROWN TORTIE

This is a combination of brown, red and cream colours with the nose leather and paw pads brown, pink, or a combination of the two.

BLUE TORTIE

This is a combination of blue and cream, with the nose leather and paw pads blue, cream, or a mixture of the two.

Chocolate Tortie Burmese

CHOCOLATE TORTIE

This is a combination of chocolate and cream, with the nose leather and paw pads chocolate, cream or a mixture of the two.

LILAC TORTIE

This is a combination of lilac and cream with the nose leather and paw pads dove grey, pink, or a combination of the two.

Lilac Tortie Burmese

SIAMESE

History

Siamese are one of the oldest and most instantly recognisable breeds of pedigree cats. There are many attractive legends that are attributed to the Siamese, but most are more than likely just the result of fertile imaginations!

Two main faults have been seen in the Siamese breed over the years, namely tail 'kinks' and crossed eyes. These are mainly due to breeding too closely, but the fables are a lot more romantic!

It is said that many years ago, in Siam, the Siamese breed were the sacred cats and were used to guard the Buddhist temples. A sacred goblet went missing, and a pair of Siamese cats were sent off to try to find the stolen treasure. After a long journey, it was finally located, and the male of the pair went back to Bangkok to relate the good news, leaving behind the female to keep guard. So vigilant was she that she would not take her eyes off the prized goblet and, just to ensure that if she fell asleep it could not be stolen, she wrapped her tail around its stem. Weeks passed before the male could return to his lady cat, during which time she had produced kittens – all of which were born with crossed eyes and kinked tails, attributed to her vigilance whilst watching the prized goblet!

Another anecdote explaining the reason for the kinked tail is that the princess of Siam used to place all her rings on her cat's tail for safekeeping overnight. One evening, the cat fell asleep and all the rings fell off and were lost. The princess decided that from then on she would tie a knot in her cat's tail so that it would never lose the rings again!

These delightful tales have helped to provide the Siamese breed with an aura of romance and royalty, but the true history of this breed is more concerned with the breeders, who, over the years, have eliminated these faults by selective breeding, introduced

Left to right: Seal, Red and Blue Point Siamese

new colour variations and, through sheer dedication, have managed to produce the beautiful, elegant and aristocratic cat that we know today.

Type

Whatever the coat colour may be, the type, size, body conformation and restriction of coloured points should be the same. There are slight differences in the standards required in different countries, and although there are now twenty colour variations that are accepted as Siamese in the UK, not all of these are considered to be so in the USA, where some are referred to as 'Colourpoint Shorthairs'.

In general, the Siamese is a medium-sized cat, that should appear long, slim and lithe but with a most definite 'muscular' feel about it. Although delicately boned, Siamese should feel heavier and stronger than they look, but at the other extreme, they should not appear to be fat or flabby. There is a definite 'proportionate' feel to a Siamese. As with any breed, the males (especially if neutered) tend to be larger than the females, and so the actual weight of the cat is unimportant so long as it is in proportion to its length and size.

The head shape, looking face on, should give the impression of a triangle topped with large, wide-set ears, tapering down to a pointed muzzle. In profile, there should be no obvious nose break, and although a slight depression can be acceptable, a pronounced bump (or Roman nose) is quite frowned upon! The eyes should be almond-shaped, with the characteristic oriental slant, and in all colour variations these should be a bright, deep blue colour, without any sign of a squint!

A Siamese tail should be long, slender and whip-like. The length of the tail should be in proportion and balance with the length of the body, and without any sign of a tail fault.

The final feature, common to all Siamese, is the quality and texture of the coat; this should always be short, sleek and close-lying, displaying a definite sheen. Any mismarkings away from the accepted areas (including white coloration around the eyes, commonly known as spectacles), discoloration in the body area (or too dark a hue) will be considered faults.

Siamese are quite susceptible to temperature, and this can be reflected in the coat colour. For this reason, the cooler parts of the body (such as the face, tail and lower legs) are those that have the darker hue and, in general, Siamese that live in warmer climes tend to have paler coats than those of cooler regions.

When viewing a litter of Siamese kittens, do remember that it may be some while before they develop their final coat colour. Siamese kittens are born almost white and, especially with the paler colours, the points do not start to show for a few weeks, while the final colouring may not be seen for several months.

Character and Temperament

Good Points

Siamese are easy to groom, with short, close-lying fur. They are intelligent and ready to accept a little 'education' from a new owner. They can be trained to walk on a lead, with a collar or harness. Siamese cats are *fun* and wonderfully entertaining. They are a companionable breed that tend to sense your moods and feelings. They are also very beautiful, elegant and glamorous.

Bad Points

Siamese are most vociferous, especially if left un-neutered, which your neighbours may not appreciate. They do not like to be left alone for any great length of time and can be destructive if left to their own devices. They are demanding and prefer to have your constant attention. They can become jealous of a new arrival, such as a new baby: have the baby first and then get a kitten! They can become very possessive towards their owner: this is less likely to be a problem if you have two Siamese.

Siamese are a beautiful and intelligent breed, but in order to get the best out of a Siamese kitten, do seriously consider the points raised above before you make a decision. In the right ownership, a Siamese will be a lifelong companion, serving you with almost dog-like devotion, but in other circumstances a kitten of this breed could drive you to distraction – and close to a nervous breakdown!

SEAL POINT

This is the original colour of Siamese, and the best known to the majority of the general public. The exact history is not known, but it is believed that they existed in Siam over 200 years ago. The first pair came to the UK in the nineteenth century, and were first seen at the Crystal Palace show in 1885. Pictures of these early Siamese bear little resemblance to the breed that we know today, other than their beautiful blue eyes and restricted coat patterning. They were considerably more chunky, with shorter, wider faces and more closely resembled the shape of the Burmese breed as seen today.

The main body should be a pale, even and creamy colour, with the darker points restricted to the face, ears (but not the back of the head or neck), lower legs and tail. These should be a deep, rich seal-brown colour, as should be the nose leather and paw pads.

Seal Point Siamese

Lilac Point Siamese

BLUE POINT

The earliest record of a Blue Point in the UK is 1894, but it is likely that they were in existence before this time. These early Blue Points were generally considered to be poor-coloured Seal Points, and many breeders preferred to forget about it, should one turn up in a litter! Over the years, they increased in popularity, but it was still not until 1936 that the GCCF gave them official recognition and their own breed number.

The main body should be a cool, glacial white without any sign of creaminess, shading to a dark, slate blue on the points. The nose leather and paw pads should also be slate coloured.

CHOCOLATE POINT

The early Chocolate Points were, in the same way as the Blue Points, considered to be pale Seal Points! The first recorded registration of a Chocolate Point was in the 1930s, and it was not until 1950 that they received official recognition.

The main body should be a pale ivory colour, with points showing a warm milk chocolate colour. The nose leather and paw pads should be pink.

Chocolate Point Siamese

Blue Point Siamese

LILAC POINT (USA Frost Point)

The Lilac Point is the result of the dilute chocolate gene being introduced to the recessive blue, producing a pale lilac colour. Lilac Points were recognised in the USA in the mid 1950s, where they were known as Frost Points – a most apt description! It was not until 1960 that the GCCF gave them recognition.

The main body should be glacial white in colour, with the points shading to a pale, pinkish grey. The nose leather and paw pads should be lavender pink.

Red Point Siamese

RED, CREAM, TORTIE, TABBY and TABBY TORTIE POINTS (USA Colourpoint Shorthairs)

These are all colours that have been man-made by crossing Siamese with other breeds to introduce new colour variations. Although they are called Siamese in the UK, they are termed Colourpoint Shorthairs on the other side of the Atlantic. Whatever the colour, their type should still be typically Siamese.

Red Point

The main body should be clear white, with the points a deep apricot red; there should be no bars or ghost tabby markings. The nose leather and paw pads should be a flesh-pink colour.

Cream Point

The main body should be clear white, with pale pinkish-cream points and, again, there should be no barring. The nose leather and paw pads should be a pale flesh-pink.

Tortie Point

Four colour variations are accepted by the GCCF, Seal Tortie, Blue Tortie, Chocolate Tortie and Lilac Tortie Points. The tortie markings should be well mingled, with the body colour showing the same tone as recommended for the 'solid' colour, i.e. a Seal Tortie should have the same body colour as the Seal Point. The nose leather and paw pads may be either the same as the solid colour, or could be flesh-pink.

Cream Point Siamese

Tortie Point Siamese

Tabby Point (USA Lynx Point)
There are six colour variations in the Tabby Points, Seal, Blue, Chocolate, Lilac, Red and Cream. The points should show clear, tabby marking and there should be an obvious 'thumb print' marking in the centre of the forehead. The body colour should reflect that of the solid colour, and may show ghost tabby markings. The paw pads should be the same as described for the solid colour, while the nose leather should be either pink, or pink edged with the solid colour.

Tabby Tortie Point (USA Torbie Point)
There are four colour variations, Seal, Blue, Chocolate and Lilac. The colouring should basically conform to that of the tabby points, being patched with cream or red. The paw pads and nose leather should likewise conform

Tabby Point Siamese (Lynx Point Siamese in USA)

Balinese

BALINESE

These most glamorous cats are, quite simply, long-haired Siamese. They were first recognised in America where, occasionally, a longhaired kitten was found in a litter. When two of these longhaired Siamese were mated together, they were found to breed 'true', so that the resulting kittens would all have long fur. It was not long before breeders realised that these cats were very beautiful and so they set out to breed from them, with the result that, in 1963, they received official recognition. However, it is only recently that they have been imported into the UK and, at the time of writing, they do not yet

have championship status, although they may be exhibited in 'assessment' classes.

Balinese should conform, as closely as possible, to the general standards laid down for the Siamese, and are available in the same twenty different colour variations. The main difference lies in the length of their fur, which should be long and silky soft and, in texture, is quite different to most Longhaired breeds and requires much less grooming. The temperament is also slightly different to the Siamese as they are much quieter in voice and less demanding, although they still do not like to be left alone for any length of time and may complain vigorously or indulge in acts of vandalism.

RECENT DEVELOPMENTS

Burmilla

Throughout the world, cat breeders are striving to produce new breeds and colour variations in their cats, and new varieties can also result from natural genetic mutations.

This last section is concerned with these developments, giving a small selection of some of the new arrivals, and also indicating which are available in the UK and USA.

BURMILLA (UK)

As the name suggests, this is the result of mating a Burmese with a Chinchilla Longhair. The original mating was a complete accident, but the resulting kittens were so delightful and sought-after that a breeding programme was set up to perpetuate the line.

The Burmilla is a Shorthaired variety that should have typical Burmese type, but with the distinctive silver ticking on the fur, a brick red nose leather outlined in black, and the mascara markings around the eyes that are typical of the Chinchilla.

More extrovert than the Chinchilla, but with a more modified character and a quieter voice than the Burmese, the Burmilla is a charming cat which is rapidly gaining popularity.

Maine Coon

MAINE COON (USA, UK)

This is a large, Longhaired breed that was first seen on the east coast of America in the state of Maine, from where it takes its name.

The Maine Coon does not have the short face seen in most Longhairs, and is generally of a more modified type; the fur is heavy and shaggy, but has an unusual silky feel to it. Maine Coons are available in many different coat colours and patterns, but the most typical is probably Tabby and White.

RAGDOLL (USA, UK)

The Ragdoll is another large, Longhaired variety and takes it name from the way it 'flops' like a rag doll in your arms when it is picked up.

A quiet and gentle cat, the Ragdoll is available in three basic coat patterns, Colourpoint, Mitted and Bi-colour, and in four different colours, Seal, Blue, Chocolate and Lilac. Although only imported to the UK in recent years, it is fast becoming a popular breed.

Bi-colour Ragdoll

SINGAPURA (USA)

This breed was first seen in Singapore where, as it roams wild and shelters in the sewers, it was commonly called the 'drain cat'. The Singapura is quite a rare breed and was first imported into the USA only a few years ago. In many respects it resembles the Abyssinian, having a similar shape, with fur that shows a distinctive ticking; the coat colour is a pale ivory, ticked with brown. The Singapura is smaller than most other breeds and has a sweet, gentle nature. It is altogether a most charming and appealing cat.

SPHYNX (USA)

The Sphynx is one of the more unusual-looking breeds of cat – it is completely bald! It is the result of a natural genetic mutation, and was first seen in America in 1966. Although it is believed that hairless cats have existed in various parts of the world for several centuries, it is only recently that a special breeding programme was developed to perpetuate this feature. Despite their lack of fur, the Sphynx does not seem to feel the cold, and is a surprisingly strong and healthy breed – with the added bonus that it does not need grooming!

Singapura

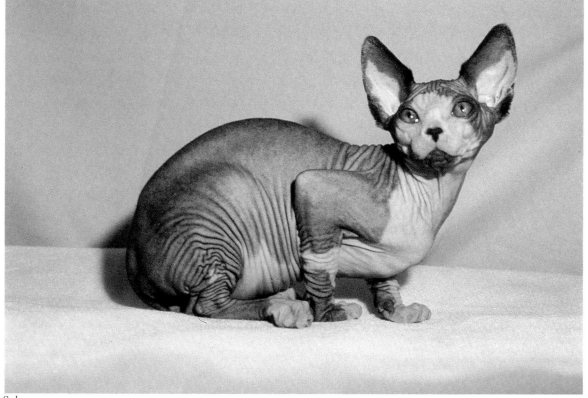

Sphynx

USEFUL ADDRESSES

We list here the official organisations of all the major cat fancies of the world, including their official or semi-official journals.

AUSTRALIA

Organisation
Co-ordinating Cat Council of Australia (CCC of A)
Box No. 4317 GPO
Sydney
NSW 2001

Journal
Royal Agricultural Society Cat Control Journal
Box No. 4317 GPO
Sydney
NSW 2001

EUROPE

Organisation
Fédération Internationale Féline (FIFE)
Sec. Mme R. van Haeringen
23 Doerhavelaan
Eindhoven 5644 BB
Netherlands

Journal
A tout Chat
(*service des abonnements* – subscriptions) BP 205
Versailles 78003

SOUTH AFRICA

Organisations
Governing Council of the Associated
Cat Clubs of South Africa
c/o Mrs M. Simpson
45 Edison Drive
Meadowridge
7800

All Breeds Cat Club
PO Box 1078
Cape Town
8000

Cat Fanciers' Club of South Africa
PO Box 783100
Sandton
2146

Eastern Province Cat Club
PO Box 5166
Walmer
6065

Natal Cat Club
100 Marian Hill Road
Ashley
Pinetown
3610

Rand Cat Club
PO Box 180
Springs
1560

Transvaal Cat Society
PO Box 13385
Northmead
1511

Western Province Cat Club
PO Box 3600
Cape Town
8000

UNITED KINGDOM

Organisations
Governing Council of the Cat Fancy
4–6 Penel Orlieu
Bridgwater
Somerset TA6 3PG

GCCF Cat Welfare Liaison Committee
Sec. Mrs Barbara Harrington
79 Pilgrim's Way
Kemsing
Near Sevenoaks
Kent TB15 6TD

Feline Advisory Bureau
350 Upper Richmond Road
Putney
London SW15 6TL

Journals
Cats
5 James Leigh Street
Manchester M1 6EX

Cat World
10 Western Road
Shoreham-by-Sea
West Sussex BN4 5WD

UNITED STATES

Organisations
American Cat Association (ACA)
8101 Katherine Drive
Panorama City, CA 91402

Cat Fancy of America (CFA)
1309 Allaire Avenue
Ocean, NJ 07712

The Independent Cat Association (TICA)
PO Box 2988
Harlingen, TX 78551

Journals
Cat Fancy
PO Box 4030
San Clemente, CA 92672

Cats
445 Merrimac Drive
Port Orange, FL 32019

Cat World
PO Box 35635
Phoenix, AZ 850969

INDEX

Page numbers in *italic* type refer to illustrations.